Edited by Amy Rost-Holtz
Designed by Maria Friedrich
Printed in China

01 02 03 04 05 5 4 3 2 1

Library of Congress Cataloging-in-Publication Data

Misuraca, Karen.
    The California coast : the most spectacular sights
& destinations / text by Karen Misuraca ; photographs
by Gary Crabbe.
        p. cm. — (A pictorial discovery guide)
    Includes bibliographical references (p. 157) and
index.
    ISBN 0-89658-481-X
        1. Pacific Coast (Calif.)—Description and travel.
2. Pacific Coast (Calif.)—Pictorial works. 3. Pacific
Coast (Calif.)—Guidebooks. 4. California—Description and travel. 5. California—Pictorial works. 6. California—Guidebooks. I. Title. II. Series.

F868.P33 M57 2001
917.9404'54—dc21
                                        2001026105

Distributed in Canada by Raincoast Books
9050 Shaughnessy Street, Vancouver, B.C. V6P 6E5

Published by Voyageur Press, Inc.
123 North Second Street, P.O. Box 338
Stillwater, MN 55082 U.S.A.
651-430-2210, fax 651-430-2211
books@voyageurpress.com
www.voyageurpress.com

*Educators, fundraisers, premium and gift buyers, publi-
cists, and marketing managers:* Looking for creative
products and new sales ideas? Voyageur Press books
are available at special discounts when purchased in
quantities, and special editions can be created to your
specifications. For details contact the marketing de-
partment at 800-888-9653.

FRONTISPIECE: *The Memorial Lighthouse stands guard on
Trinidad Bay (in Humboldt County).*

TITLE PAGE: *Sunset lights the surf at Point Lobos State Reserve.*

TITLE INSET: *A foggy morning in Santa Barbara harbor.*

TABLE OF CONTENTS: *Early morning sunlight creeps across the
crags at Rocky Point near the Carmel Highlands of Monterey
County.*

DEDICATIONS

To Leah, Laurel, Melati, Rachel, Acacia, Wyatt, Alex, Duncan, Cooper, and their generation. Lovers of the outdoors, wanderers on the bluffs and beaches, they are a hearty band of adventurers, striding into the future as loving stewards of the California coast. —KM

To Connie: Your unconditional love, understanding, and support keeps me in constant and humbled awe; without it, my contribution to this book would not have been possible. And to my son Brandon, because one great first deserves another. —GC

PHOTOGRAPHIC NOTE

All of the images created for this book were made with a 35mm SLR camera system. Specifically, I used either a Nikon 8008s or N90s camera body. I have a variety of lenses that range from a 24mm wide-angle lens to a 300mm telephoto lens, of which all are Nikon, save one Sigma 28–70 zoom lens. For images that required the use of a flash, I still use a trusty old Nikon SB-24 Speedlight, often connected to the camera using a SC-17 extension cord. In most cases, my camera was attached to a Gitzo Carbon Fiber 1228 Mountaineer tripod, topped with a Slik Standard Ball Head II and a Quick Release plate by Really Right Stuff. The only filters I use are a Circular Polarizer and a pair of Split Neutral Density Filters by Singh Ray. The ND filters are used to control the amount of light reaching part of the frame, without adding, altering, or changing the color, hence the term "neutral." All images have been recorded on professional transparency film, mostly Fuji RVP ASA 50, Fuji RFP 100, and Fuji RFP II. Film processing was done exclusively by The New Lab in San Francisco. —GC

The CALIFORNIA COAST

The Most Spectacular Sights & Destinations

Text by Karen Misuraca
Photography by Gary Crabbe

A Pictorial
Discovery Guide

Voyageur Press

CONTENTS

FOREWORD
by Jean-Michel Cousteau

California is a fabled land. And of all its storied landscapes, the coast is for many the most inspiring. From rugged forest promontories to sandy beaches, it boasts a diversity that is hard to match anywhere on earth. From small, Hispanic-influenced farming towns to the cosmopolitan bustle of San Francisco and Los Angeles, it is host to a blend of cultures not seen since the days of ancient Rome.

Karen Misuraca is our guide to this fascinating world, introducing us to the state's natural and human history in a truly inspired feat of storytelling. The California she shows us is not always the same as we see on television. It is more honest and more true to the way we really live here. In the words of its residents, as quoted by the author, the coast comes alive as a place of good fortune, resilience, and constant wonder.

But, above all else, it is a place of incredible natural beauty. Misuraca and photographer Gary Crabbe move beyond the glamour of California's culture to capture the grandeur of its natural endowments. Like many writers, she finds gems off the beaten track. More importantly, I think, she directs the reader to the gems ON the beaten track, the wondrous unfoldings of nature that happen all around us, each and every day. As we who live here know, you don't have to be a trailblazing John Muir to find solace and renewal in nature. All you need is to look around you. And Misuraca tells you where, when, and how to do it.

For all its bounty, however, California's coastline is an environment under siege. The state is now home to over 30 million people, and more arrive every day. Perched precariously on the edge of this human tide, the fragile ecosystems of the coast are under constant pressure from development, resource extraction, and even tourism. By learning to appreciate the treasures around us, in books such as this, we can take a significant step toward protecting them for ourselves and those who follow, assuring that our descendants will also be able to enjoy a piece of the California dream.

President of Ocean Futures Society and one of the world's leading marine environmentalists, Jean-Michel Cousteau has spent his life exploring the oceans aboard the research vessels *Calypso* and *Alcyone*, and communicating to people of all nations his love and concern for our water planet. The eldest son of the late ocean explorer Jacques-Ives Cousteau, Jean-Michel takes education as his life's work, especially of young people. The nonprofit Ocean Futures Society (www.oceanfutures.org) conducts marine education programs and research, and focuses public attention on marine issues of critical importance.

FACING PAGE AND ABOVE: The western edge of the North American continent plunges into the Pacific Ocean, creating a rich habitat for marine life, such as sea anemones.

ℐNTRODUCTION

Since European explorers sailed from the Old World to the New in the sixteenth century, the western edge of the North American continent has lured travelers with a siren's song, promising golden days of abundance and ease. From the wave-lashed rocky coves and cool, deep forests of her northern shores, to her southern sunny, sandy beaches, the California coastline has embraced her suitors in breezy arms, surrendering, with a mild countenance, the harvest of her seas and the fruits of her lands.

Spanish conquistadors in wooden ships, pioneers in prairie wagons, and gold seekers on horseback arrived on these shores with high expectations. They found the means to turn dreams into reality to the extent that they acceded to the landscape and the climate as determinants of their fate.

Then, as now, the lives of Californians are marked by the moods of the sea, the forces of nature, the landscape, and the unique geologic features of the coastal regions.

THE BREATH OF THE SEA

A mighty weathermaker, the Pacific Ocean sends currents of moist air up against the rumpled coastal mountain ranges, creating a Mediterranean climate of gentle, damp winters and warm, dry summers, with summer fogs common in some areas. The frequent rains that occur in the north are absent, for the most part, south of Point Conception, where the north-south run of the coastline turns east-west, creating an unofficial dividing line.

Extreme weather occurs only on the extreme North Coast, the target of gales that seem to race straight from Siberia. The average annual rainfall in Crescent City, near the Oregon border, is seventy-four inches, while in San Diego, near the Mexican border, it rains less than ten inches a year. Midway between them, San Francisco receives about twenty inches. On the Lost Coast near Eureka, where moisture-laden clouds bump into sheer mountainsides, one hundred inches of rain drenches fir and redwood forests, feeding icy waterfalls and streams.

Changeable is the word for weather on the Central Coast between San Francisco and San Luis Obispo Bay. Clouds come and go, and even the densest fog usually burns off by midday. The color and pulse of the sea frequently shift, often in the span of an hour or two. The best months for travel on the entire coast are May and June, September and October, when seas are generally calm and skies are clear.

FACING PAGE: *On the constantly evolving edge of the continent, the craggy coves of the North Coast are guarded by sea stacks and broken arches, remnants of an ancient mainland.*

ABOVE: *Some of the richest tide pools on the Pacific Coast are found at Fitzgerald Marine Reserve in San Mateo County.*

THE ROMANTIC NORTH

Mountains meet the sea on the North Coast, a land of big rivers, evergreen rain forests, and irregular shoreline scrubbed by a raucous surf. With few inhabitants, it's a romantic place, largely untrodden and still open to true adventure and discovery.

Carved into coves and small bays, the northern littoral is sculpted by wave action. Some pristine beaches are nearly inaccessible below precipitous cliffs, notably those on the Lost Coast of Humboldt County and in Big Sur, near Monterey.

Travelers come north, "up the coast," for the wild beauty and the feeling of isolation, where the only footprints on a beach may be one's own, and brooding groves of redwoods stand in utter, primeval silence, as they have for over a thousand years. Wrapped in mists and pummeled by storms, northern seacoast towns are small and snug, picturesque with Victorian- and Gold Rush–era buildings. Their people are known to possess a fierce independence, more fierce than ever now that their historic enterprises of commercial fishing and logging are dramatically curtailed due to vanishing resources.

SOUTHERN SKIES

South of Point Conception, sun from a brilliant, overexposed blue sky warms the soul all year-round, save the occasional midwinter day. Golden beaches stretch for literally hundreds of miles, a great, convex, sandy shore separated by narrow mountain ridges from the intense heat of the vast Mohave and Sonoran deserts in the interior.

Drawn inexorably to the sea, 80 percent of the state's population lives within thirty miles of it. Soaking up sun and taking cloudless skies for granted, most of the people are clustered in sprawling, congested Southern California. Endowed with few mists and fewer mysteries, San Diego, Los Angeles, and Ventura Counties are dependably moderate in temperature, confirming Ralph Waldo Emerson's comments in his 1871 *Journal*: "The attraction and superiority of California are in its days. It has better days, and more of them, than any other country."

CONTINENTS COLLIDE

Each pebbled cove and river inlet, each quaint fishing village and harbor has a story to tell. From an old Indian footpath to a Victorian-era lighthouse to oyster farms in a sheltered bay, life on the California coast ebbs and flows according to the whims of the sea, and sometimes, the whims of a moving landmass.

Here on the edge of the Pacific Rim, the shoreline cleaves two continental plates, the North American Plate—which is the mainland—and the Pacific Plate, which is, for the most part, under the ocean. The turbulent geological history of the Pacific Coast began more than 250 million years ago when these plates began to collide. Sinking underwater and pushing steadily eastward, the Pacific Plate burrowed under the North American Plate, causing the Coast Range and the Sierra Nevada Range to wrinkle and uplift, building volcanoes and inland seas that eventually became the vast, dry valleys of today.

These continental plates, and those along the entire edge of the Pacific Rim, continue to grind against each other. On the California coast, the Pacific Plate slides ever northward against the dry land. This movement occurs along notorious earthquake faults, like the San Andreas Fault that runs beneath the San Francisco Bay area and the San Jacinto Fault in Southern California. When the plates move even a fraction of an inch, the earth shudders and buildings creak and crack and occasionally fall down, a phenomenon that Californians seem to take in stride.

Los Angeles is on the Pacific Plate, west of the faults, and San Francisco is on the North American Plate. Over the next ten million years, after a steady succession of earth movements, the two cities will be neighbors.

THE VERNACULAR

Notwithstanding the occasional temblor, a great deal of vintage architecture survives. Built during the Gold Rush of the mid 1800s, thousands of gabled, turreted, gingerbread-trimmed Victorian mansions are the "Painted Ladies" of San Francisco, Eureka, and other North Coast towns.

Some of the first houses built in California were the whitewashed adobes on the "Path of History" in Monterey State Historic Park. Familiar images of Southern California are the red-tiled roofs and arched loggias of Santa Barbara and San Diego, evidence of Spanish colonization. Influenced by Spanish and Mexican *rancho* traditions, the modern California ranch-style house originated in Southern California.

ALONG PACIFIC COAST HIGHWAYS

Drawn irresistibly to where the blue Pacific meets North America, today's Californians turn to the coast

A warm horizon dims over a silver sea off Bodega Head in Sonoma County.

The waters are warm off Laguna Beach, one of Southern California's most popular stretches of sand.

for refreshment of their minds and bodies. Visitors come here by the millions from throughout America and the world to see famous landmarks and historical sites and to enjoy the weather. On the longest coastline of the continental American states, more than one hundred California beaches, parks, preserves, and monuments are easily accessible from the meandering coastside routes, Highway 1 and Highway 101. Five national parks or national recreation areas are contiguous to the coast, as are four national marine sanctuaries.

Only here are the redwoods and sequoias, the world's largest and tallest living things. Only here do hundreds of people walk across a golden bridge, every day, rain or shine, just to say they did it once in their lives. Only here do more than fifteen thousand California gray whales parade offshore for months at a time, close enough to be seen without binoculars. Only here are the humanmade miracles and entertainments of Hearst Castle, Disneyland, SeaWorld, Santa Cruz Boardwalk, and Monterey Bay Aquarium.

Surfers flock to Huntington Beach—"Surf City U.S.A." They ride the rollers at Steamers Lane in Santa Cruz and the notorious fifty-foot breakers at Maverick's, near Half Moon Bay. Pleasure craft sailors berth ten thousand boats in Newport Harbor, the second largest yacht harbor in the world.

Birdwatchers laden with cameras and tripods creep silently along the shores of the natural estuaries of Morro Bay and Elkhorn Slough, precious sanctuaries for birds and ducks migrating along the Pacific Flyway. Kayakers paddle Tomales Bay at Point Reyes National Seashore, peering down into the clear waters for glimpses of bat rays and baby sharks. Scuba divers descend into kelp beds off the Channel Islands, keeping their eyes peeled for Stellar sea lions, harbor seals, and sea otters. Bikini-clad blondes play volleyball on Venice Beach. Babies play in the warm, azure waters of La Jolla Cove.

Families set up umbrellas on Butterfly Beach in Santa Barbara and pull on their windbreakers at Land's End above San Francisco Bay. Lovers hide among the dunes of Salmon Creek State Beach in Sonoma County and take it all off at Black's Beach in San Diego. Solitary walkers atop the soaring cliffs of Big Sur peer across the Pacific to faraway places, while quiet groups of tourists and locals gather every evening to watch the sunset on Carmel Beach. Magnetic in its beauty and invigorating atmosphere, just the sight and scent of the Pacific Ocean repairs the spirit.

"For many people, romance and the movies are what attract them to the California coast," said Bill

Native grasses bend in the breezes on a North Coast beach near Arcata.

Spring Cleaning at the Beach

Marin County resident Nancy Palozola found an abandoned boat heater, soft drink cans, and plastic junk on Muir Beach one April day in 2000. She was one of thousands of volunteers participating in California Coastal Cleanup Day, an annual event that focuses attention on ocean and shoreline pollution from Mexico to the Oregon border. On that same April day, beachcombers picked up enough garbage from six miles of Orange County beaches to fill ten garbage trucks.

Organized by the Center for Marine Conservation, Cleanup Day involves more than 50,000 people, who pick up nearly 640,000 pounds of debris and recyclable materials. Fishing line, strapping bands, plastic bags, and six-pack rings are among the most common abandoned items, although a wide variety of things turn up. From Sonoma County beaches, a big-screen television was hauled away, along with a cow costume, the rear end of a car, and a message in a bottle from a ten-year-old girl looking for a pen pal.

Most of the junk comes from beach-goers, from recreational and commercial boaters, and from storm drains, or it is carried by wind, streams, and rivers out to the beaches and ocean. Once entangled in debris, marine animals, birds, and fish have trouble eating, breathing, and swimming, and they often mistake plastic for food, feeding it to their young.

On California Coastal Cleanup Day, Nancy Palozola picked up junk on Muir Beach in northern California, while beachcombers in Orange County cleaned up enough trash to fill ten garbage trucks.

Ahern, director of the California Coastal Conservancy, a nonprofit organization that acquires shoreline access and protects wetlands and watersheds. He said, "People want to see where *Kojak* or *Baywatch* were filmed, or where Elizabeth Taylor and Richard Burton illicitly kissed in *The Sandpiper*. . . . Other people come for the rugged, isolated hiking on the Lost Coast, or driving the stretches of the legendary Pacific Coast Highway that have been featured in numberless automobile ads. For visitors who come here to swim and surf, it is usually a shock to find out the California current that washes our coast, is, well, quite cold.

"My advice is to get away from roads and parking lots, and hike or stroll along the spectacular trails in the state parks which stretch along a quarter of the coast, or even across private property where we and other agencies have acquired easements, the right of the public to walk to and along the coast. Bring binoculars and check out the birds on the wetlands, rivers and creek estuaries, and on the beaches."

CALIFORNIANS AND THEIR COAST

Other than the indigenous peoples, all Californians are recent immigrants, and unlike populations with long, shared histories, they are constantly reinventing themselves. Common among them is the untiring pioneer spirit of the New World and an inclination to rush toward the opportunities of the untried future in the West.

A Monterey County native and former congressman and White House chief of staff, Leon Panetta said of Californians, "We are more free spirited than other Americans, who seem attuned to a more stratified, traditional way of life. Californians appreciate the quality of life we have here, the beauty of the land. Everyone knows that living in California is the full measure of being a human being. I have always felt that with all our natural resources, we have the crown jewel of beauty."

The attitudes and the mien of Californians are different in the north than in the south, and over the years, serious proposals have been put forth to split the state into two parts. Humanity tends to take over in metropolitan Southern California, where wealth and political power are concentrated, while the balance tips toward nature in the northern reaches. Northern Californians resent sending their fresh water south, and many loathe the congestion and what they consider to be overdevelopment in the southland. Bonding the bronzed denizens of the sunny south with the hardy souls on the state's northern end is an intense love of the ocean, not only as a playground but also as part of the world's marine environment. Nowhere in America are citizens more dedicated stewards of their seacoast.

A resident of the Central Coast and founder of the Ocean Futures Society, an organization dedicated to exploring issues affecting the ocean, Jean-Michel Cousteau is the son of pioneer oceanographer, Jacques Cousteau. Speaking of the unique character and value of California's coastal waters, Jean-Michel said, "This coastline is distinguished by high biodiversity and by an enormous concentration of marine life. It is a very healthy coast, although affected by a massive amount of people.

"Nonetheless, the strength of the biodiversity is such that, provided you give it a chance, it recovers fast. We have seen it with the kelp forest being able to take all kinds of punishment. Whether manmade or in nature as with 'El Nino,' it does recover.

"The population of California . . . really has a huge impact on marine life, not only directly by what we take, but indirectly by the runoffs and (our) shaping and reshaping the coastline, thereby destroying marine habitat. . . . This coast receives a lot of punishment. Nonetheless, it remains very, very rich."

From the redwood forest preserves to the National Marine Sanctuaries, the California coast is in the never-ending process of being restored, rescued, and recovered by Californians, intrepid "tree-huggers" and nature-lovers.

"The coast is never finally saved, it is always being saved," said Peter Douglas, executive director of the California Coastal Commission, an agency charged with establishing shoreline access and defending thousands of miles of coastline from commercial and private development. He said, "Effective stewardship requires constant vigilance and active citizen involvement. Californians care passionately for their coast . . . a fragile, finite resource requiring everyone's care and attention."

California Coastal Commission

Californians love their coast—nine out of ten go to the beach at least once a year, and they are among the most fervent of environmental activists, demanding public access to the entire shoreline.

"The coast is California's geographic heart and soul," said Peter Douglas, executive director of the California Coastal Commission, an agency established in 1976 to defend against loss, damage, and development. The commission's major accomplishments have been, in Douglas's words, ". . . the things one cannot see and that are not readily measurable—wetlands and ocean waters not filled, public access and agricultural lands not lost, scenic land and seascapes not spoiled by development, new subdivisions that did not occur . . . new offshore oil and gas development that did not happen."

From the Oregon border to Mexico, travelers encounter the commission's distinctive wooden signs, showing two bare feet under an ocean wave, heralding hundreds of public entry points to footpaths and roads, often through private property, leading to the shore and to bluff-top trails. The state claims ownership of property above "mean high tide line," meaning that visitors have the right to walk on a wet beach—any beach.

Pescadero State Beach in San Mateo County is two miles of tidepools, dunes, and trails. Sea lions and the seagulls like it here, as do the anglers who catch steelhead and salmon in Pescadero Creek.

Chapter 1

Ɲorth Coast

Redwood Country

Crescent City to the Lost Coast

Left: *A World Heritage Site, Redwood National Park is the last sizeable stand of the California coastal redwoods, the world's tallest living things.*

Above: *A windswept house clings to an eroding cliff top on the rugged Lost Coast in Humboldt County.*

The sea and the land do not meet peacefully on the North Coast, nor is the weather always welcoming to humans. It is, however, a perfect climate for California coastal redwoods, the world's tallest trees, in fact, the world's tallest living things. So unique and magnificent are the redwood forests that much of the Northern California coastline, extending a few miles inland, bears the title "The Redwood Empire."

Until the 1920s, when one in every thirteen Americans had acquired an automobile, this coastline and the redwoods were largely unseen, except by Native Americans, by hunters and trappers, and by loggers cutting the timber needed for the booming city of San Francisco during the Gold Rush.

All of Northern California was dramatically affected by the discovery of gold in the Sierra Nevada Mountains in 1848. Towns and cities grew up practically overnight and needed timber for building. As it was easier to move timber by sea than overland, communities were established on the shore of every navigable bay and many coves. These were quickly settled by loggers, millworkers, and supporting businesses. Of the hundreds of lumber mills in operation during the last half of the nineteenth century, only a handful exist today.

Washed by thundering waves in the winter, damp and foggy in the summer, the North Coast has superlative spring and fall weather, with warm days and cloudless, cerulean skies to match the sea. Wintertime is for romantics who love the drama of a tumultuous gale and the warmth of a fireplace while rain pelts the roof and stiff winds drive smashing surf into the rocky pinnacles offshore. Thriving in the moist climate is a breathtaking, true wilderness, most of it readily accessible—luxuriant forests of redwood, ponderosa pine, Douglas fir, and Sitka spruce; the magnificent Smith and Klamath river valleys; Humboldt Bay and the pristine Lost Coast.

More than in any other region in California, the rhythm of daily life on the North Coast is determined by the climate and the mood of the sea. Rugged indi-

vidualists, physically strong North Coasters wrest their livelihood from a frigid, unforgiving ocean, pulling in cod, salmon, tuna, and crab. Or they bulldoze roads into the forests and drag out trees as big as skyscrapers, to be milled into lumber.

Editor of the *Daily Triplicate* in Crescent City, Fred Obee said, "There is a certain majesty to the storms, and it can storm like crazy. But, we don't hole up. Often people will drive to the waterfront to watch the action. As isolated as we sometimes feel, we are generally very self-reliant and traditional, and really love the outdoors, hunting, fishing and kayaking, and of course, the incredible redwoods. Our economy is changing from almost entirely fishing and logging to an emphasis on tourism and retirement."

NORTHERN HAMLETS

The small towns of Klamath, Smith River, Orick, and Crescent City are not tourist destinations in themselves so much as base camps for exploring national and state parklands. A small jewel box of a town born in the Victorian era, and a mecca for birdwatchers, sport fishers, and antiques collectors, Eureka is the southern hub of Redwood Country, located at the edge of the second largest deepwater port in California—Humboldt Bay.

Rocked by tremendous storms most winters, Cres-

The moon sets as rosy dawn lights fishing boats in Crescent City harbor.

Battery Point Lighthouse gleams in the evening light over Crescent City.

cent City was stricken by a tsunami in 1964, and the downtown drowned beneath twelve-foot waves. Today the town is in good shape, with seafood cafes, canneries, and fishing boats providing a colorful backdrop. Visible from Highway 101 is the busy fishing port and a few historical sights. The circa 1850 Battery Point Lighthouse and museum are stranded on a tiny island at high tide; when waters recede twice a day, visitors trod a century-old pathway to see old lighthouse lenses, Native American relics, and logging artifacts.

A pleasant, meandering curve of sand and rocks on the edge of town, Pebble Beach ends at Point St. George. Obee said, "From here north, the character of the shoreline changes into a wild, windy beach that goes on for miles. Everything imaginable washes up on the sand—piles of shells, driftwood, fir and redwood planks, and logs. And, in the late winter, huge flocks of Aleutian geese gather near here in the fields and in the Lake Earl freshwater lagoon. There is even an annual Aleutian goose festival."

Seasons are marked by celebrations and harvest festivals, important events for the isolated communities. At the height of the Dungeness crab season in February, locals at the Crustacean Festival and World Championship Crab Races line up their prickly, pink and red contestants and excite them into action by clapping, yelling, and stomping alongside the racetrack. Then the feasting begins on spicy crab *cioppino*; cold, cracked crab with melted butter; crab cakes; crab Louie; and barbecued and baked crab.

Held on the Yurok Indian Reservation, the Salmon Festival in June features traditional dancing, drumming, games, and logging skills contests, then culminates in a huge salmon barbecue. For centuries, the Klamath River area has been the hunting and fishing grounds of indigenous tribes— the Tolowa, the Yuroks, and the Chilula. The superior Yurok canoes, hollowed out from trunks of fallen redwoods, were highly regarded by neighboring tribes, who traded goods for them. A few thousand Yuroks live along the Klamath River today, on a forty-mile strip running inland from the mouth of the river.

Wild rhododendrons bloom at the mouth of the Klamath River valley. A few thousand Native American Yuroks live on a forty-mile strip running inland from the mouth of the river.

Believed by Indians of the past to be haunted by evil spirits, the "Trees of Mystery" near the town of Klamath are a strange collection of redwoods and spruce trees that have grown into distorted shapes, with twisted branches and contorted trunks. The Trees are guarded by a forty-nine-foot-tall carving of the mythical, burly logger, Paul Bunyan, and his seventeen-ton blue ox, Babe. Huge chain-saw sculptures are on view here, too, from bears standing on their hind feet and cubs climbing up tree trunks to eagles in flight and whales' tails.

THE REDWOOD PARKS

Dedicated in 1968 by President Lyndon B. Johnson, Redwood National Park shelters one half of all remaining old-growth redwoods on earth and actually encompasses three state parks: Prairie Creek Redwoods, Del Norte Coast Redwoods, and Jedediah Smith Red-

woods. Covering more than 100,000 acres along forty miles of coastline, and including rivers, streams, hiking trails, campgrounds, and scenic roads, it is one of the most magnificent and least visited of America's national parks.

A dense canopy of overlapped branches shields the redwood forest floor from all but narrow beams of sunlight, and there is little woodland growth, save moss, ferns, and lichen. In the understory where the sun breaks through and in the openings on the edges of creeks and rivers, wildflowers and shrubs flourish. Huckleberries and thimbleberries bear bright red fruit. White fairy bells; pink milkmaids; the creamy white, three-lobed western trillium; and carpets of yellow redwood violets are sprinkled beneath spring-flowering Pacific dogwood. California bay, madrone, and live oak trees provide red and golden accents in the fall.

Illuminated by slanting shafts of sunlight, redwood groves are often described as cathedrals, and some people say they have a spiritual experience among these trees. According to Denise Delle Secco, a state park interpretive specialist, "Most people say the same thing when they see the redwoods for the first time— 'awesome.' They do silly things like stand in the middle of the road or walk in circles. It's a very physical and emotional, even a mystical experience. People actually get quite overwhelmed and even tired at the sight of the tremendous trees in their impressive, natural environment."

Flourishing in drizzle and damp, these silent giants from the age of the dinosaurs exist only here and on a few scraps of land in a narrow corridor extending to the Monterey Peninsula. Although redwoods began to appear on the earth only twenty million years ago, because of their tremendous breadth and height, and the look of the mysterious, mist-wrapped forests, the redwood groves resemble a primordial world in which one expects to see pterodactyls flying by. As it is, black ravens do swish through the branches from time to time, shadows in the ancestral gloom.

High in the redwood forest canopies, a microclimate exists that is very different in temperature and solar exposure than at the base of the trees. In the windy treetops are osprey nests and habitat for two endangered birds—spotted owls and marbled murrelets.

Rather than build their own nests, the owls inhabit broken crowns of trees and openings in rotted trunks. About twenty inches long with white speckles on fawn- and brown-colored feathers, they have a sharp hoot that sounds like a small dog barking. Cutting roads through mature forests where northern spotted owls nest has resulted in the birds near-extinction.

A robin-sized seabird related to the puffin, marbled murrelets raise their young high in old-growth redwoods and Douglas firs. They fish in the sea during the day, retreating at twilight to their moss-lined nests, crying *keer-keer-keer*. Sensitive to the slightest changes in their ecosystem, these and other species live and reproduce only in old-growth forests.

A few miles northeast of Crescent City where Mill Creek meets the Smith River, Jedediah Smith Redwoods State Park is the northernmost of the state redwood parks. The park is named for the legendary explorer, Jedediah Strong Smith, who discovered the Smith River and blazed a trail from the Great Salt Lake through the Mojave Desert and the San Bernardino Mountains into California in 1826. Two years later, he rafted down the Klamath River to the Pacific and survived an Indian massacre, only to be killed by

Shade-loving ferns flourish beneath the canopy of a redwood forest. Thriving on drizzle and damp, these silent redwood giants from the age of the dinosaurs exist only in a narrow corridor on the California coast.

Comanches in 1831.

Mixed with the redwoods in this forest are old-growth Sitka spruce, western hemlock, Douglas fir, and Port Orford cedar. This is true wilderness, witnessed by the presence of black bears, mountain lions, and bald eagles. The Simpson-Reed Nature Trail, less than a mile long, traces the park's northern border, connecting to a footbridge and the half-mile trail to Stout Memorial Grove, a kingdom of immense redwoods— one is 340 feet high and 22 feet in diameter.

The most popular destination in this park is at the end of an old logging road. Lady Bird Johnson Redwood Grove honors one of the leading environmentalists of the twentieth century, a woman who redefined the institution of First Lady. Standing beneath the towering trees, she said, "Here on the North Coast of California, the ancient and awesome redwoods make their last stand. The Latin name for the great redwoods—*sequoia sempervirens*—means 'the tree that never dies.' Let us be thankful that in this world, which

World's Tallest Living Things

Coming upon the giant trees in 1769, Spanish explorer Fray Juan Crespi named the California coastal redwoods *palo colorado*, or red tree. In 1847, the official Latin name, *sequoia sempervirens*—meaning "ever-living"—was bestowed in honor of the beloved Cherokee chief, Sequoyah.

Old-growth redwoods exist in a few pockets of land entirely within a narrow, five-hundred-mile strip of the Pacific coast between the Oregon border and the Santa Lucia Mountains south of Monterey, in a mild, moist microclimate of fog and rain. In the dryer months, they draw moisture from the air through their boughs, up to a thousand gallons of water a day, one molecule at a time, an adaptation that explains, to a degree, why they are able to live thousands of years.

Descendants of gigantic evergreens that grew during the age of the dinosaurs and related to the massive giant sequoias (*sequoiadendron gigantea*) found in Kings Canyon, Sequoia, and Yosemite National Parks, redwoods are not as wide nor quite as long-lived as sequoias, although they are considerably taller. Their sapless, cinnamon-colored bark, as much as a foot thick, gives the redwood its distinctive fluted appearance and contains tannin that successfully resists pests, diseases, fire, and floods.

Alone among cone-bearers, redwoods have cones so tiny that they seldom work their way down through the duff to the forest floor. Instead, new trees sprout from the trunks or roots of established trees. Given their tremendous height—some over three hundred feet tall and twenty feet in diameter—their root systems are surprisingly shallow, only six to eight feet, with no tap root. Massing their roots together in groves is another reason the trees are strong enough live as long as two thousand years.

The richly charactered, deeply colored wood is prized for long-lasting decking, outdoor furnishings, and decorative interiors, and these qualities have been its downfall. Once there were two million acres of redwoods in California; now, there are scarcely ninety thousand. The virgin stands have been largely decimated, primarily by clear-cutting that destroys not only the trees but also many of the creeks, rivers, and hillsides that served as wildlife habitat. Although national and state parks protect the remnants of the primal northern forests, logging is still allowed in some parks.

offers so few glimpses of immortality, these trees are now a permanent part of our heritage."

FISHING ON THE SMITH

On three forks of the Smith River in Jedediah Smith Redwoods State Park, school-bus-sized boulders and towering redwoods line the banks. Swimming holes are many and fishing is legendary. Savvy anglers know to cast inside the river bends, in fast, shallow riffles. Fishing is done by driftboat or from the banks, as far up as the little town of Gasquet, although the favored area seems to be near the fork's bridges, downriver.

One of only two percent of America's rivers that are free-flowing and pristine enough to be included in the National Wild and Scenic River System, the Smith is the largest undammed river in California. It is said to be the cleanest river in North America.

An avid fisherman, angling editor of *Western Outdoor News*, Rich Holland, finds nirvana on the banks of the Smith River. He said, "The big difference between this and other California rivers is the abundance of King and Coho salmon, steelhead, and cutthroat trout. Steelhead, which is actually sea-run rainbow trout, can be well over twenty pounds, and salmon over fifty pounds are not uncommon.

"Most rivers are degraded by agriculture, logging, and gravel extraction, and although the Smith is also under heavy pressure from man's touch, the population of wild and hatchery fish remains high, for now. This is a healthy river, the only river in the state to allow a wild fish take. The limit now is one fish per day per angler, either hatchery or wild."

Holland recommends wintertime, from December to March, for the best fishing. He said, "It rains a lot up here, but even after a winter storm when the river blows out and turns brown, it is often fishable again within just a day or two, primarily due to the gravel bottom. The minute it starts to clear, trucks line up at the Highway 101 bridge near the water tower and 'the plunkers,' as they are called, start catching fish."

Just south of Crescent City and the Smith River, a scenic hike in Del Norte Coast Redwoods State Park starts on a section of the original Highway 101, which was abandoned in 1935 and is now called the Last

26

Chance Trail. Running above the shore, the trail affords views of the city and Enderts Beach, dropping down into Nickel Creek Canyon and climbing up, steeply, to the headwaters of Damnation Creek, where dense stands of spruce, fir, and redwood grow, some a dozen feet across at the base.

PRAIRIE CREEK AND THE TALL TREES

Down the coast, six miles north of Orick, Prairie Creek Redwoods State Park was set aside in 1920. A place of surreal beauty, it comprises twelve thousand acres of magnificent coastal redwoods, seventy miles of trails, and one of the most spectacular beaches on the Pacific Coast.

The crown jewel of the park, Fern Canyon is a mile-long gorge splitting a coastal bluff and walled by fifty-foot cliffs lavishly draped in sword ferns, lady ferns, horsetail, and five-finger ferns. The creamy-white bells of fairy lanterns hang in clusters. Monkeyflowers are flickers of sunny yellow through the dense green. In the wettest areas of the trail, boardwalks and wooden bridges traverse the creeks and marshes. Nearly a foot long, the Pacific giant salamander creeps among the golden globes of skunk cabbage.

The Fern Canyon loop trail connects with a path to Gold Bluffs Beach, which is also accessible by unpaved road. Bursting out of the canyon as it meets the sea are a profusion of emerald green ferns, scattered in the spring with wild strawberry blossoms, blue and yellow lupine, and pink rhododendron.

High sandstone cliffs frame eleven miles of driftwood- and log-scattered sand beaches and dunes, and the vigorous surf here creates a vaporous, low-level atmosphere that mingles with the foamy, breaking waves. Adding to the extraordinary allure of Gold Bluffs Beach are grazing Roosevelt elk, which often create a dramatic tableau on the cliff tops and along the road that runs above the shoreline.

HUMBOLDT BAY AND EUREKA

North and south of Humboldt Bay, the largest embayment between San Francisco and the mouth of the Columbia River, Highway 101 passes an extraordinary array of spectacular beaches and rocky coves, marshy lagoons and small bays, wild river valleys and evergreen forests. Redwoods meet the sea on the isolated Lost Coast, where few people have explored the mountainous shoreline and deep forests of King Range.

A small jewelbox of a town, born in the Victorian

As this dense rainforest has seldom, if ever, echoed with the sound of an ax or a saw, Prairie Creek is primeval in its mossy elegance. It may seem familiar to movie-goers who saw The Lost World: Jurassic Park; *backgrounds for the lumbering dinosaurs were filmed here.*

Herds of Roosevelt elk live at Prairie Creek and on the Lost Coast.

era, Eureka is laid out right on the bay. Blocks of elaborate, ginger-bread-trimmed homes, hotels, and historic buildings were built between 1850 and 1904, and more than ten thousand of them remain—more per capita than any other California city. A circa 1888, Eastlake-style extravaganza with an unusual diamond- and square-paneled frieze and porthole cutouts, "Abigail's Elegant Victorian Mansion" is an inn owned by Lily and Douglas Vieyra, who welcome guests to stay in antiques-filled rooms, watch vintage movies, and wander in a garden of nearly two hundred antique rose bushes. A former seaman, wilderness ranger, historian, and movie extra, Doug is multi-lingual and an expert on area attractions.

A museumlike sawmill and job shop that makes custom trim for Victorian buildings, Blue Ox Millworks uses the same machines that created the originals. Owner Eric Hollenbeck recovered abandoned machinery from closed-down mills and literally from the briar patches of Mendocino County. Visitors teeter on catwalks overlooking the workshop below, watching as artisans turn columns, carve rosettes, and form wooden gutters and gewgaws. Surrounded by a beautiful wetlands wildlife sanctuary, the Blue Ox has also re-created a loggers' camp and set up a bird-viewing station.

For an overview of the busy harbor and the wildlife in Humboldt Bay, passengers cruise on the M.V. *Madaket*, a wooden, steam-driven ferry built in the 1920s and the oldest passenger-carrying commercial vessel in the United States. Historical and natural sights are explained as the ferry passes oyster farms, a plethora of fishing and pleasure craft, the third largest colony of harbor seals in the West, and one of few remaining egret rookeries existing anywhere.

In Eureka's Old Town, Humboldt Bay oysters and fresh seafood are served in opulent, candlelit surroundings at the Hotel Carter. Oenophiles make pilgrimages here to taste the rare vintages offered on the wine list, which is regularly singled out as one of the best in the country. Besides renovating the century-old hotel, the owners erected a replica of a San Francisco

For the annual World Championship Great Arcata to Ferndale Cross-County Kinetic Sculpture Race, fantastical, handmade, people-powered contrivances are driven, dragged, and floated over roads, mud flats, sand dunes, Humboldt Bay, and the Eel River.

Victorian mansion across the street, outfitting it with marble fireplaces and four-poster beds.

Humboldt County is home to more than eight thousand artists, and Eureka has been called one of the best small art towns in the United States. A library building donated to the town by Andrew Carnegie early in the twentieth century now anchors the local art world as the Morris Graves Museum of Art, dedicated to a former resident and famous artist.

Across the Samoa Bridge on Woodley Island, the Samoa Cookhouse has been operating since 1885 and is the last surviving lumber camp cookhouse in the West. Family-style meals are served at long, oilcloth-covered tables with charmingly mismatched chairs. Huge loaves of bread, cauldrons of soup, platters of ham and roast beef, and big bowls of salad and vegetables accompany the entrees, followed by wedges of homemade pie. Prices are reasonable and little kids eat free.

Behind the cookhouse are the empty streets of an old logging company town and breezy walking and biking trails in the Samoa Dunes Recreation Area. Fluttering like pieces of torn white paper, flocks of egrets fly above their rookery in a grove of cypress trees. With much of its undeveloped fringe designated as wildlife refuge, Humboldt Bay includes one of three

Speckled with gold, the sand from Gold Bluffs Beach was mined in the 1800s.

remaining large natural estuaries in the state (the others are Elkhorn Slough in Monterey County and Morro Bay on the Central Coast).

On the north end of Humboldt Bay, Arcata Marsh and Wildlife Sanctuary is best seen in the mists of early morning, when stilt-legged herons stand motionless, hidden in the bulrushes. Coots mutter and green-winged teals squawk in the narrow canals. Red-winged blackbirds prattle loudly as they cling to the tall reeds. Their sharp talons alert for live prey, northern harriers work the marsh all day, browsing for voles and ground squirrels on the pastureland edges of the marsh. Northern river otters are often seen swimming briskly along in the canals, their heads barely above water, searching for fish, frogs, and turtles, their favorite foods.

Ornithologist and director at LBJ Enterprises, a biological consulting firm, Robert Hewitt said, "The last two weeks in September are thought to be our best for rare birds. In 1985, the only oriental green finch yet recorded in North America south of Alaska was seen here. A white-winged tern from Central Asia turned up in 1998, the first time it was recorded on the West Coast. It is quite spectacular with a solid black body, white wing flashes and tail, and bright red bill and legs. It would not have been expected again in decades, but presumably the same bird put in a return, showing in August a few months later at the marsh, never to be seen again."

The marbled godwit is celebrated annually at Godwit Days in March, bringing hundreds of birders from across the country. According to Hewitt, "The godwits breed in Alaska, and this is the farthest north they winter in any numbers on the West Coast. . . . At least twenty thousand show up in the wintertime."

Arcatans are serious about maintaining natural habitat for birds and for themselves. Although it is entirely unapparent, Arcata Marsh is actually a wastewater reclamation project and, in fact, a model for the nation of how to combine wastewater treatment with recreation and wildlife preservation. The city also owns and sustainably manages a redwood forest, which is threaded with walking paths and preserves habitat for the endangered spotted owl.

Just south of Eureka, thousands of birds and ducks migrate through the grasslands and fresh- and salt-water marshes of the Humboldt Bay National Wildlife Refuge, stopping to feed and rest, to breed and overwinter. Twenty-five thousand black brants fly here from their nesting grounds in the Arctic on their way to Baja, California. Alongside the Hookton Slough footpath, tundra swans and northern pintails swim in the ponds and tidal channels in the wintertime, as do Canada geese and cinnamon and green-winged teal in the summer. Black terns circle and hover above the cattails, swooping to scoop up the damselflies. Great blue and black-crowned night herons, and great and snowy egrets, tiptoe stiffly about the mudflats, stabbing small fish.

One of more than five hundred national wildlife refuges, the Humboldt Bay preserve is true wilderness, notwithstanding its easy access. Visitors set up cameras and binoculars on tripods, and follow trails from along the brackish waterways to birding sites in the Loleta and Eel River Bottoms. The "bottoms" between Eureka, Loleta, and Ferndale are flat pasturelands near the sea, crisscrossed by a network of country roads between Highway 101 and the ocean. From the

Twist and Spout!

The sight of a fifty-ton gray or humpback whale, thirty-five feet long, bounding up out of the Pacific Ocean, can be the highlight of a visit to California. On a whale-watching expedition by powerboat offshore or from a high vantage point on land, there is a good chance of seeing the creatures from December through January, and from March into May, along the entire California coast.

About twenty thousand California gray whales migrate annually from summer feeding grounds in the Bering Sea to Baja, California, and back, a thirteen-thousand-mile round trip. Heading for warm-water lagoons, they breed and bear their offspring, returning north a few months later with their babies, hugging the shoreline, usually within a half mile and sometimes as close as four hundred feet.

Ten of the twelve known whale species can be spotted off the Pacific shore; the most common is the gray. Blue and humpback whales migrate farther offshore, in deeper waters, from July through October.

Some of the prime locations for whale sighting from the mainland are Redwood National Park, Gold Bluffs Campground, MacKerricher State Park, Point Arena, Point Reyes, and many points on the Mendocino and Sonoma County coastlines.

Harvesting much of the shrimp, Dungeness crab, salmon and cod consumed on the Pacific Coast, a fleet of five hundred fishing boats docks in Humboldt Bay.

Standing four stories tall, aloof above Old Town Eureka, the William Carson Mansion is a combination of Queen Anne, Italianate, and Eastlake styles that took one hundred men more than two years to build for a lumber baron in the late 1880s.

The rising sun warms the air above Arcata Marsh on Humboldt Bay. March and April are the best months of the year to see exotic birds and ducks. Migrating birds are in the thousands in midwinter.

Fire and Light

"The environment is important to everybody who lives here, regardless of their income or politics," said John McClurg, proprietor of one of Arcata's several sustainably operated businesses. A small fishing and logging town on the northern edge of Humboldt Bay near the mouth of the Mad River, Arcata has since the 1970s been a model community when it comes to preserving the environment.

McClurg operates Fire and Light, producing tableware made from recycled glass. From bins of mayonnaise jars, beer and soft drink bottles, pickle pots, and castoffs from a stained glass factory, Fire and Light craftspeople load tons of broken glass into 4,200-degree furnaces, then transform the molten glass by hand, piece by piece, into dinnerware and decorative pieces in luminous, jewel-tone colors of plum, coppery orange, pale celery, and cobalt blue. By calling ahead, visitors can watch the spectacular process, from trash cans full of broken glass to the fiery meltdown and the nimble, rather dangerous, pouring of red-hot glass into molds.

"Arcata has one of the oldest recycling centers in the country, and to avoid sending our glass far away for reuse, and to add value and create jobs right here, some local people got together literally in someone's living room and decided to work with a local glass artisan to produce salable glass items," McClurg explained. "Now, we have nearly thirty employees and sell our products all over the country."

John McClurg, proprietor of Fire and Light

village of Loleta, a quiet lane heads west towards an arm of the Eel River at the edge of the estuary and to Cock Robin Island Road, where mudflats attract masses of plovers, swans, and curlews.

THE LOST COAST

Thirty miles south to Leggett, Highway 101 forsakes the mountains and the rugged coastline, bypassing what is arguably the only true wilderness remaining directly on the California coast, the sixty-two-thousand-acre King Range National Conservation Area. Known as the Lost Coast, the area is accessible by a handful of back roads and hiking trails. Rising from sea level to four thousand feet in less than three miles, the terrain is steep and rocky.

Hikers on the Lost Coast may hear Roosevelt elks thrashing saplings and polishing their antlers on small tree trunks. Weighing upwards of one thousand pounds and outfitted with racks of five-foot-long antlers, the bulls are crabby and territorial during mating season in the fall and early winter, and an encounter with a bull and his harem on the trail can be a breath-taking experience.

A taste of the lonely, pristine wilderness is found on two-lane Mattole Road, between Ferndale and Weott. A tortuous corkscrew called the "Wild Cat," the road winds through a dense coniferous forest, plunging downhill past green cattle ranches and falling-down barns to the village of Petrolia, where a five-mile, usually passable road leads to the mouth of the Mattole River at the ocean.

Wildly beautiful and often wildly stormy, the gravelly river estuary is a collection point for thirty-nine tributary streams, and a resting and breeding area for migrating birds and shorebirds. Semipalpated plovers race along the littoral, whistling *tu-wheet, tu-wheet.* Arriving from their breeding grounds in Alaska, sooty

Covered with a drizzly forest of Douglas fir, big-leaf maple, and alder, most of the Lost Coast is frequented only by mule deer, a few bobcats, and hardy backpackers.

ABOVE: *The Bear River empties into the Pacific Ocean on the largely uninhabited Lost Coast.*

RIGHT: *The marbled godwit winters on the Lost Coast and the entire shoreline of California.*

black turnstones overwinter here, probing for crabs and sand fleas and uttering a distinctive rattle, *kreeer*. Warblers, finches, wrens, and wrentits trill and click in the lush riparian vegetation, guarding their down-lined nests. In the deeper waters of the estuary, a colorful array of red-breasted mergansers and other diving ducks swim about with common loons and long-necked, red-eyed Western grebes.

Moist sea air bumps into the high barrier of the King Range, making this one of the wettest spots on the Pacific Ocean, receiving more than one hundred inches of rainfall annually. May to September, dry days as warm as eighty-five degrees often alternate with frequent dense fog—good hiking weather.

EEL RIVER REDWOODS

On the east side of Highway 101 in the Eel River Valley, 60 percent of the tallest trees can be seen along the thirty-one-mile Avenue of the Giants in Humboldt Redwoods State Park. Turnouts, parking areas, and short loop trails into the forest make these giant trees the most accessible in the state.

The largest and one of the least visited of state parks, in part because it encompasses several small towns, the state park is divided by the highway and has no main entrance. Most of the park lies to the west and is reached by leaving the Avenue of the Giants and taking Mattole Road to Rockefeller Forest, a ten thousand-acre tract of virgin redwoods alongside Bull Creek. The forest contains some of the tallest trees that exist. The former champion sequoia Dyerville Giant, about 362 feet tall, fell here in rain-saturated ground in the spring of 1991. And although the new champ, a 369-footer, was discovered in an isolated grove in Montgomery Woods near Ukiah, behemoth contenders stand tall in Rockefeller Forest.

State Park Interpretive Specialist Denise Delle Secco said, "Few visitors to the redwood parks go any farther than the roadside or more than a quarter mile from the visitor's centers. Even though the backcountry is easily accessible, most people never see the parks as they were when first created, never experience the grandeur of the trees and the virgin wilderness that has been so carefully saved for them. I call the redwood parks 'living museums.' It's like going to the Smithsonian, a once in a lifetime opportunity."

The Saving of Luna

To save the life of a two-hundred-foot-tall, ancient redwood tree near Stafford, just north of Humboldt Redwoods State Park, a young woman, Julia Butterfly Hill, braved the wrath of a corporate giant, a powerful logging company. For 738 days, she lived in the damp, cold arms of the tree, which she named Luna, on two six-by-six-foot platforms, never setting foot on the ground during that time. Food, fuel, mail, and phone batteries were hauled up in a bucket. Celebrities visited her, and the national media covered the ongoing ordeal.

Throughout the stormiest winter in Northern California's recorded history, Hill withstood all-night spotlights and bullhorns wielded by company security, survived buffeting by a giant logging helicopter attempting to drive her down with wind blasts over one hundred miles per hour, and refused to give up her 180-foot-high perch. She said, "When I first came out here in the summer of 1997 and saw the intensity of the devastation of clear-cutting, the mud-slides and the practices of the lumber companies, I was ignited. I had to do something. Here I could be the voice and the face of this tree, and for the whole forest that could not speak for itself."

Hill finally descended from the tree in December, 1999, when the lumber company agreed to forego clear-cutting in that area. Hill gave the company $50,000 raised from contributions and earmarked for educational programs.

Describing Luna, Hill said, "She is truly massive, two hundred feet tall, and once was much taller, before her top was blasted off by lightning. She has two caves burned out by forest fires, one on either side, and another in the top canopy. Even though she is old and decaying, she furnishes nutrients for a tremendous amount of moss and lichen, huckleberry, ferns, and salmon berry. Chipmunks came every day while I was there, and two northern flying squirrels lived in the tree. I try to remind people that old-growth trees don't exist only to survive themselves, they are vital shelters and providers for dozens of species of plants, animals and birds. New life is constantly beginning here."

In 2000, Luna was seriously vandalized by an unknown person, who cut nearly half-way through the tree's fifteen-foot-wide base with a chain saw. Hill said, "The fate of Luna and the remaining redwoods depends on the Creator and the people of this planet."

Chapter 2

THE SONOMA-MENDOCINO COAST

Fort Bragg to Bodega Bay

LEFT: *In marine terraces and steep cliffs, the Coastal Range tilts into the Pacific Ocean on the dramatic shoreline of Sonoma and Mendocino Counties.*

ABOVE: *Dad and son peer into tide pools at MacKerricher State Park near Fort Bragg.*

Spring, with its breezy, blue-sky days, brings wildflowers to the meadows that lie nearly a thousand feet above rocky coves running from Bodega Bay to Fort Bragg. Baby lambs and newborn calves romp in the high grass while newborn gray whales and their mothers gambol and leap a few hundred feet offshore. Summer, a time of warm weather with foggy mornings and nights, finds tourists sightseeing in tiny fishing villages and Victorian logger's towns. In the fall, the weather is perfect, crystal clear and brisk. Winter is for lovers, when magnificent storms turn beaches into treasure chests of driftwood, shells, and other discoveries washed up by the pounding waves.

Much larger in the 1800s when it bustled with loggers and miners, the entire town of Mendocino is a historical preservation district of early Cape Cod–style and Victorian-era homes and steepled churches. Point Arena is prime whale-watching country and the site of a notorious point of land that lured ships to their demise in decades past. A chain of beautiful beaches stretches north from Bodega Bay, a small fishing village where seals, sailboats, windsurfers, and thousands of birds share a harbor.

Beautiful Bodega

Although the town was founded in the 1870s, most of the buildings of architectural interest in Bodega Bay are circa 1910, early California Craftsman–style bungalows. A handful of seafood restaurants and a few shops and inns are scattered around a large, protected

Around each curve of Highway 1 is a postcard view of a sandy or pebbled beach, jagged with crumbling seastacks, and washed by a foamy surf.

harbor, where pleasure boats from around the world come to anchor, dodging sea lions and harbor seals.

Day-trippers and seagulls observe boxes of fresh albacore, salmon, mussels, and sand dabs being unloaded from boats on the wharf, home base for nearly three hundred commercial fishing boats. When the Dungeness crab season starts in November, the Tides Wharf and Restaurant features crab *cioppino*, and the place is crowded with diners lingering at sunny window tables that overlook the action of the wharf and the harbor. Attracting big crowds of visitors in April is the Bodega Bay Fisherman's Festival, which starts with the blessing of the fishing fleet and a decorated boat parade, followed by a big outdoor fair and lamb and oyster barbecue.

Clamming in the tidal mudflats and windsurfing in the harbor are two popular activities. The freshwater wetlands and salt marshes attract a wide variety of shorebirds and waterfowl—such as sanderlings, plovers, herons, cormorants, marsh wrens, and red-winged blackbirds—and even pond turtles and the endangered salt marsh harvest mouse.

On the outer rim of the harbor, Bodega Head is an immense slab of granite, a promontory overlooking the open sea and about forty miles of coastline. Whales are easily sighted from here in December and January and in March and April. Among the highlights of the park trails are the San Andreas Rift Zone as it passes from beneath the ocean up into the mainland, a cave with a freshwater spring, and what is known as the "Hole in the Head," the foundation of a nuclear power plant that was never built due to the protests of the Northern California citizenry.

Sonoma Coast Beaches

From Bodega Bay north to Jenner are sixteen miles of what is known as the Sonoma Coast State Beaches. Salmon Creek Beach is a broad, two-mile expanse of sand edged with grassy dunes, some as high as 150 feet. Boardwalks cross the vast network of dunes, giving easy access and protecting the native grasses.

A small, pretty, wind-sheltered beach with abundant tidepools, and the best of the Sonoma Coast Beaches for shelling, Shell Beach is the trailhead for the Pomo Canyon Trail, an old Indian route that rambles up and over the hills. Passing through knee-high meadows, over creeks, and under shade trees, the footpath leads to a small redwood forest, rewarding hikers with a windy view of the Pacific. The path goes on another mile or so through oak and bay woodlands and grasslands to the Russian River.

Magenta-colored ice plant paints the dunes at Salmon Creek Beach in Sonoma County.

Berry bushes and crushed shell mounds along the trail were left by early Miwok, who paddled dugout canoes in the river and hunted whales and sea lions along the coast. They collected wild berries, greens, clams, and mussels, and tossed handmade nets to catch salmon and herring.

THE RUSSIAN MEETS THE SEA

The Russian River winds down from the mountains of Mendocino County through redwood canyons and past sandy beaches, old apple orchards, and thousands of acres of vineyards, sliding calmly to the Pacific Ocean at Jenner. In the mid 1800s, tourists from San Francisco rode ferries across San Francisco Bay and hopped onto a narrow-gauge railroad to reach summer resorts on the river. The arrival of the motorcar and the decline of lumbering caused towns along the river to fall into a deep sleep for a few decades. The town of Guerneville never missed a beat, however, thriving through the Big Band era when the Benny Goodman and Harry James bands performed, and weekenders thronged the dance halls. In the 1970s, the tremen-dous growth of wineries in the area began a new era of tourism, and now more than fifty wineries welcome visitors on the back roads of the Russian River Valley.

Canoers and kayakers paddle down the river from Healdsburg to Jenner, where it empties into the sea. Although a dangerous place to swim, Goat Rock beach is popular for beachcombers and shore and freshwater fishing at the mouth of the river. Seals like it, too. A large herd is often sunbathing and surfing, and in the spring, they give birth to their pups away from deep ocean predators. More than two hundred species of birds and ducks frequent the tidal flats, including great blue herons, white and brown pelicans, gulls, ospreys, and peregrine falcons.

SEA RANCH

About twenty miles north of Jenner, most travelers drive along Highway 1 enjoying the view, never realizing that several hundred homes are hidden in the meadows and evergreen groves on both sides of the road. One of the most restrictive residential developments ever built in California, Sea Ranch is charac-

Goat Rock is a landmark on the Sonoma Coast. The beach here is a favorite for driftwood collecting and shore fishing.

The Russians Came, the Russians Left

Meandering north along the Sonoma County coast, scenic Highway 1 relaxes briefly from its relentless tortuous turnings into a straight stretch. Appearing on a wind-scraped clearing is a high wooden stockade with a tower topped by a Russian Orthodox cross. Here, in 1809, twenty-five Russians and eighty Aleut fur hunters arrived to harvest the silky pelts of sea otters and seals and to grow wheat and vegetables for Russian outposts in Alaska. Three years later, they built a small settlement of hand-hewn log barracks, a blockhouse and homes, and a jewel of an Orthodox church.

Named Fort Ross, for the country *Rossiya*, the settlement was surrounded by imposing redwood bastions and a bristling line of forty-one cannons, just in case the Spanish or the English decided to pay a call (they never did).

The compound is now Fort Ross State Historic Park, one of the most fascinating and well-developed historic sites on the North Coast. Several of the buildings and the church are replicated in a magical greensward above the Pacific. The "crib" style architecture uses hand-adzed logs notched together and fastened with oakum, a jute rope and tar combination. Inside the buildings are yard-wide floorboards and perfectly preserved rifles, pistols, tools, furniture, and old photos.

Hiding below the fort is a lovely, protected cove, where shell collectors browse the beach. Walking trails head both north and south of the fort along meadowy headlands and a creek lined with laurel and willow trees. A few apple trees and a Russian cemetery survive from the old days.

On "Living History Day" at Fort Ross in July, costumed docents re-enact a day in 1836, making candles, threshing wheat, cooking, and engaging in noisy musket and cannon drills. The docents spin stories of the Russians, ultimately about three hundred or four hundred of them, and the indigenous Kashaya Pomo Indians. They took well to each other, intermarrying and trading guns and saddles

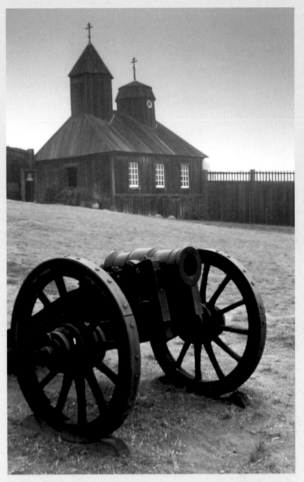

Cannons guard the replicated Russian Orthodox church at Fort Ross State Historic Park.

for food and baskets. Unfortunately for the seal and otter populations that once swarmed in great numbers along the entire coastline, the settlers hunted them nearly to extinction, taking up to one thousand seal pelts in some months. (A threatened species, today sea otters are found mainly in Monterey Bay and south along Big Sur.)

When their crops failed and otters were no longer abundant, the Russians offered to sell the fort to the Spanish in 1839. The Spanish declined, and John Sutter purchased the fort, removing most of the contents to his sawmill in the foothills of the Sierra Nevada. Sutter's business partner, James Marshall, discovered gold in the mill race in 1848, setting off the great California Gold Rush.

terized by untouched open space and architectural restraint. Widely scattered, naturally weathered, unpainted wood houses on the headlands and hillsides are barely visible. None are more than two stories tall, some have sod roofs, and the architectural style is simple and contemporary. Vehicles are out of sight, fences are absent. Native grasses and trees are unfettered by non-indigenous flora. The result of these extraordinary regulations is acres of headlands and wooded hills that look much as they did a century ago.

"Opposition to Sea Ranch in the 1960s, a former sheep ranch that had been purchased for development of 5,200 homes, became a rallying cry for environmental activists throughout the state, and eventually resulted in the establishment of the California Coastal Commission," said Peter Douglas, executive director of the Commission. "This spectacular ten-mile reach of windswept Sonoma County coast became the focus of an intense struggle. . . . Ultimately, Commission action secured . . . beach accessways, a three-mile blufftop trail, a reduction by half of density and protection of key views from Highway 1."

From the Sea Ranch Lodge, trails lead to several beaches and along the bluffs. Paved roads on the east side of the highway wind through a redwood, madrone, fir, and pine forest. Wild azaleas, rhododendrons, and irises bloom in the spring. Wild mushrooms are rampant and colorful.

MUSHROOM HUNTING AT SALT POINT

"The best time of year to pick mushrooms is from the end of September to early December," said mushroom naturalist Charmoon Richardson, proprietor of the Wild About Mushroom Company. He guides fungi fanciers on expeditions near the Sea Ranch and into Salt Point State Park, one of the few public lands where it is legal to pick wild mushrooms.

"At Salt Point, we hike into the hills in the pine belt, looking for the King Boletus—often known as porcinis or French ceps. These are the big ones, wider across than the top of a five-gallon bucket," he said. "We also find pumpkin-colored and golden chanterelles, oyster mushrooms, matsutakes, hedgehogs, and black trumpets, the best eating of the more than two thousand types of mushrooms that grow in the Pacific Northwest."

Salt Point State Park is a microcosm of the beauties of the North Coast, encompassing seven miles of beaches, rich tidepools, steep cliffs, and verdant, tree- and shrub-covered hills. Above Highway 1, the park rises from grasslands into dense growths of Douglas fir, oak, madrone, and second-growth redwoods. Topping the ridge at one thousand feet is a forest of miniature cypress and pines, their gnarled, ghostly gray arms tickled with maidenhair fern—one of a handful of pygmy forests on the North Coast. Hikers and horseback riders often encounter deer and the occasional coyote and bobcat. Black bears are known to venture down from the untracked mountains into the park, although visitors seldom see them.

Some of the prettiest walking paths in northern California trace the bluffs of the park above surf-splashed, rocky inlets and coves distinguished by sandstone outcroppings as artfully carved and positioned as a modern sculpture garden. Purple and yellow bush lupines and bright yellow Scotch broom crowd into the dry gulches. Creeks and waterfalls are lush with ferns. Large numbers of cormorants nest at Stump Beach Cove, where driftwood piles up. At Gerstle Cove, harbor seals sun themselves on the rocks. Tidepools are bright with red bat starfish and ochre sea stars, mussels, and gooseneck barnacles. The vivid red antennae of tiny hermit crabs flash among a waving garden of anemones. Purple urchins and lapis-blue sea stars compete for attention with giant Pacific octopi. They are not so giant, really—only about a foot long at maturity, with arms that change from brown to bright red on a moment's notice—but they can be disconcerting to a barefoot tidepool explorer.

SHIPWRECKS

The Point Arena fishing pier juts 330 feet out into the sea from the edge of a cove, creating a good vantage point for whale-watching. Rock fishing, abalone diving, and crabbing are the main activities here, along with tidepool exploration at the base of the cliffs.

The original wooden fishing pier at Point Arena was dramatically smashed to pieces in a 1983 storm, along with all of the buildings in the cove. In a café on the pier, the Galley at Point Arena, are photos of the rip-roarin' squall. The sunny café serves hearty seafood chowders, snapper sandwiches, homemade pies, and Dungeness crab in season.

On the hill above the pier is the most elaborate of

several Victorians in the tiny town. The Wharf Master's Inn was built in the 1870s for the men who watched over the port until the 1920s. A fantasy of turned posts, scroll brackets, and fancy window moldings, the house was prefabricated in San Francisco and shipped here as a kit. Next door, the Coast Guard House is a classic early California Arts and Crafts–style house. Built in 1901 as a lifesaving station, it is now a romantic bed-and-breakfast inn.

MENDOCINO

In the mid-nineteenth century, loggers from New England sailed around Cape Horn to the North Coast, a voyage of about six months. Misty river valleys, untracked mountains thick with massive evergreens, and a pristine seacoast were true wilderness then, inhabited only by indigenous tribes and a few fur trappers. The first redwood mill in California was erected on the Big River below Mendocino, and there was work for all, cutting timber and milling lumber for the booming Gold Rush city of San Francisco. By 1878, the population grew to twenty thousand—compared to one thousand today—and plenty of ruckus was raised in nineteen saloons and more than a dozen pool halls and "fast houses." According to the local newspaper, "the one bastion of good Christian morals in a town of loggers" was the Temperance House, which is today the Mendocino Hotel.

Today, looking across the Big River at the postcard view of Mendocino with its white, clapboard storefronts, Victorian-era mansions, and distinctive water towers, it is easy to imagine horse-drawn carriages tied up in front of Temperance House and ladies with parasols sweeping along the boardwalks in long gowns.

Mendocino remained rough-and-tumble until the 1930s, when the lumbermen left due to the dwindling supply of redwoods. The town languished for decades, only to be reborn as an art colony and eventually a tourist destination. Ships captains' mansions are now bed-and-breakfast inns, and in the saltbox cottages are quaint shops and art galleries guarded by picket fences that scarcely hold back rampant old-fashioned gardens. Clematis vines and honeysuckle clamber unchecked over water towers and tilting barns; wild strawberry creeps up the fenceposts, bursting into white blossoms in the spring.

A visitor's center for the state park and a museum, Ford House, the home of the Mendocino Historical Society, is a good place to gain perspective on how the town is laid out. A scale model of the 1890s shows dozens of tall, wooden water towers that existed at that time. More than thirty of the towers, some double- and triple-deckers, remain in the skyline today. A Whale Celebration is held at Ford House in March, at the height of the annual migration, featuring "whale walks" and whale-sized hot dogs.

Anchoring Main Street like a dowager queen from Victorian times, the Mendocino Hotel is museumlike

Erected in 1870, then re-erected after the 1906 San Francisco earthquake, the 115-foot Point Arena Lighthouse is the all-time best location for California gray whale watching. Black oyster-catchers and cormorants wheel over the offshore rocks, and sea lions and harbor seals are often seen in the waters just south of the point.

Looking across the Big River to the white, clapboard cottages and the New England–style, steepled churches of Mendocino.

the coastline. Volatile North Coast weather is the topic of conversation at Wind and Weather, a shop in the Albion Street water tower selling weather instruments, vanes, and sundials. Sea- and shorebirds flock and swirl outside a tiny store called Papa Birds, where outdoor feeders attract hundreds of feathered creatures.

Between high bluffs on the south side of Mendocino, the Big River meets the sea in a driftwood-strewn beach. Great blue herons share the river valley with ospreys and wood ducks, harbor seals and river otters. Above the mouth of the river, canoers and kayakers paddle seven or eight miles upstream past riverbanks lined with fir and redwood groves, wildflowers and wild rhododendrons. Deer are often seen, and occasionally a small black bear. The trick is to time a canoeing expedition up the river when the tide is coming in and make the return trip as the tide goes out.

EXPLORING STATE PARKS

Among other popular outdoor recreation in the Mendocino area is abalone diving in the cove at Van Damme State Park. Here, also, is the weird Pygmy Forest, where trails lead to sword-fern canyons and a spooky woods of dwarf, lichen-encrusted cypress, pines, and other bonsai-like plants and

with nineteenth- and early twentieth-century art and furnishings. The dark, rich tones of Oriental rugs are a warm backdrop for the bank teller's booth, which serves as the registration desk; it is topped with a Tiffany lamp, circa 1928. From the Victorian love seat to the carved, fluted, and scrolled mahogany sideboards, the lobby alone is worth a look. The catbird's seat in this town is at a window table in the hotel bar, overlooking the crashing surf.

Another good spot from which to view the ocean and seabirds is in Out of This World, a shop on Main Street where high-powered telescopes are trained on

trees. A fifty-year-old cypress may be only eight inches tall and have a trunk less than one inch in diameter. Experienced guides conduct sea kayak tours from Van Damme beach, in and out of sea caves and along the rocky edges of nearby coves.

Sea caves are among the unique geological features to be explored just up the coast at Russian Gulch State Park, along with a thirty-six-foot waterfall and a beach popular for rock fishing, scuba diving, and swimming in the chilly waters. The Devil's Punch Bowl, a two-hundred-foot-long tunnel with a boisterous blowhole, is visible from the headlands.

The sunset bathes the Little River Inn in a golden glow.

Tales of the Little River Inn

A thirty-nine-year-old lumberman from Maine, Silas Coombs heard tell of golden opportunity in California. So in 1856, he sailed from New York to Panama, slogged on foot across the Isthmus of Panama, and gained passage aboard another ship to San Francisco.

Observing the building boom going on in the city, he realized that the gold at the end of his rainbow lay in the forests of the North Coast, where red-barked trees were said to be three hundred feet tall and twenty feet across. He walked from San Francisco as far north as the Little River, which seemed a likely outlet for logs from the mountains, and built a mill and a wharf in 1863. By 1880, he was a rich lumber baron with a beautiful wife and a home befitting his wealth.

The local newspaper described Coombs's Victorian mansion as "a very nice residence, with conservatories, verandas and all modern improvements of an eastern home."

A piano that came around Cape Horn in those early days stands in the vestibule of the home, which is now the Little River Inn, owned and operated by Coombs's great grandchildren, Dan Hervilla and Susan McKinney.

On a bluff above Van Damme State Park, on 225 acres of redwoods and gardens, the inn has been a weekend destination for San Francisco Bay Area residents since 1939. As fancy as a white wedding cake, the house is embellished with lacy white trim, intricately cut-out banisters and turned columns. Purple wisteria and trumpet vines cascade over the veranda, and heirloom roses bloom in the salt air.

From its opening until well into the 1960s, the dining room menu always included fresh abalone, and it came only one way—poached—in other words, taken illegally. The patriarch of the family at that time, Ole Hervilla, was notorious for picking abalone right off the rocks in the cove at the mouth of the river. Guests at the inn often got into the act by helping to row Ole's skiff in return for a free meal.

By 1960, the jig was up. Ole and his wife were ordered to appear in court on charges of taking and selling abalone for commercial purposes. Since it was impossible to empanel a jury of locals, as they were all friends and frequent abalone diners at the inn, an informal agreement was reached, prohibiting Ole from his lawless harvest.

Sitting in the White Water Bar of the inn, a cozy hideaway adorned with family photos and antique logging equipment, Ole wrote a poem:

> Oh, some folks boast of quail on toast
> because they think it's toney;
> But bring me a pail of gin
> and a tub of Abalone.

At Jug Handle State Reserve, an "ecological staircase" rises from the littoral to about five hundred feet, with each level of beautiful marine terrace one hundred thousand years older than the one below, creating a unique opportunity to see geologic evolution. The plants and trees change from terrace to terrace, from wildflowers and native grasses to wind-strafed Sitka spruce, Douglas fir, second-growth redwoods, and pygmy forests of cypress and bishop pine.

FISHING AND BEACHCOMBING IN FORT BRAGG

A lumbering and commercial fishing town since 1857, Fort Bragg is a port at the mouth of the Noyo River. Several coastal and forest state parks and good river fishing make this a headquarters for exploring the southern end of Redwood Country. Fort Bragg is also the departure depot for the famous California Western Railroad Skunk Train.

Hauling logs to sawmills in the 1880s, the Skunk Train—actually several historic diesel and steam trains—now delivers provisions to people living in isolated places along the tracks and takes tourists on daytrips to Willits and back. The trains rock alongside Pudding Creek and the Noyo River, through redwood forests, crossing thirty bridges and trestles over deep gulches, passing idyllic glades and meadows. Passengers sit inside the railcars or stand on open-air platforms, enjoying the sight and scent of the evergreens and the whistles and creaks of the train. The Skunk Train got its nickname from the old gasoline engines that prompted people to say, "You can smell 'em before you can see 'em."

Just north of Fort Bragg, at MacKerricher State Park, are two freshwater lakes stocked with trout, and equestrian, mountain biking, and hiking trails that wander throughout the bluffs and wetlands. A family of harbor seals is in residence at Laguna Point. Stretching the length of the park, the paved Old Haul Road, a former logging road, provides great access to ocean views and high sand dunes.

Just north of Fort Bragg, MacKerricher State Park is eight miles of beach, dunes, and tidepools, a gentle contrast to the rugged nature of most North Coast beach parks.

Built as a hospital in 1915, the Grey Whale Inn is a four-story, redwood clapboard landmark in Fort Bragg. One of the guest rooms, Bear Harbor, was once the labor and delivery room, and the sink is where many of the town's current residents were given their first bath.

In the heyday of lumbering in the mid 1800s, there were three lumber mills, three hotels, and several saloons at Noyo Harbor.

GORGEOUS GARDENS

One of the loveliest walks on the California coast is just south of Fort Bragg in the Mendocino Coast Botanical Gardens, the only public gardens in the continental United States that front the ocean. Summer's heat is softened by frequent fog, and winters are damp with no extremes in temperature. This combination exists in only a few other parts of the world: on the coast of South Africa around Cape Town, on the southern coasts of Australia and Chile, and in parts of the Mediterranean.

A horticultural bounty results. The gardens are a lush universe of native plants and trees, many from faraway places. Of particular note are the wild and cultivated rhododendrons and azaleas, both of which bloom in great clouds of magenta, pink, yellow, red, and white. When the "rhodies" are in their glory from March to May, wildflowers are at their blazing best in the headlands, misted by spray from the billowing breakers.

An hour's stroll, or a cruise in a golf cart for those less able, turns up unusual succulents, camellias, a marsh, and organic vegetable gardens. Wild white and purple irises and lilies of the valley illuminate a shady creek and a mossy fern canyon. From November through January, Japanese maples and heathers are aflame with color.

OLD FISHING PORT

At day's end, sea lions bark and pose on the wooden piers at Noyo Harbor, waiting for the return of the fishing boats laden with salmon and albacore. Home to a fleet of trollers, the harbor is a good place to rent a rod and cast for rockfish off the piers or the rocks. Herring is the popular bait, set on gold-colored hooks decorated with colored beads to attract the fish. This is the best place on the eighty-mile Mendocino County coastline for queasy-stomached passengers to take a whale-watching cruise, because the animals are usually sighted within less than thirty minutes.

On the hillside above, a lumber tycoon's mansion was handcrafted in 1868 by Scandinavian shipbuilders. Today, it is an inn, where Oriental rugs and vintage photos are warm accents against the redwood board and batten paneling and heartwood fir floors. There is one, and only one, drawback to staying at the Lodge at Noyo Harbor: The sea lions on the piers sometimes bark loudly early in the morning as the fishing fleet heads out into the morning mist.

Chapter 3

San Francisco and Marin County

Point Reyes to Ocean Beach

LEFT: *Spanning the entrance to the largest protected bay for a thousand miles, the Golden Gate Bridge connects San Francisco with the Marin Headlands.*

ABOVE: *Swathed in fog, Muir Woods National Monument shelters the last remaining virgin redwood groves in the Bay Area.*

Sixty miles long, twelve miles wide, San Francisco Bay is the largest protected coastal bay for a thousand miles. Fed by the mighty Sacramento River, plus the San Joaquin, the Petaluma, and the Napa rivers, the bay was discovered in 1769 by Spanish explorer José Francisco de Ortega. Overjoyed to find the vast, sheltered harbor and plenty of fresh water, the Spanish built a garrison and a mission church. While the small port town grew slowly, the Mexicans routed the Spanish, and the Americans raised the stars and stripes in 1846.

"If California ever becomes a prosperous country, this bay will be center of its prosperity," wrote Richard Henry Dana in *Two Years Before the Mast* (1834). "The abundance of its wood and water, the extreme fertility of its shores, the excellence of its climate, which is as near to being perfect as any in the world . . . affording the best anchoring grounds in the whole western coasts of America, all fit it for a place of great importance."

San Francisco was still a tin pot settlement when, in 1848, "Gold!" rang out in the Sierra Nevada foothills, a hundred miles inland. Within weeks, the bay began to fill with wooden ships and the hills with tents and hardscrabble shacks. The population zoomed from five hundred to forty thousand in a year, while goods streamed in to supply miners and budding capitalists from Virginia City to the Klondike, and gold and silver flowed through San Francisco banks.

Abandoned ships were pulled ashore for use as hotels and warehouses, and the party was on. There were ten "49ers" to every woman in 1849, denizens of the "Barbary Coast," the red-light district on the waterfront where grub, whiskey, and personal services were cheap.

Educated, worldly European immigrants profited greatly during the Gold Rush and, a decade later, from the discovery of the world's richest silver deposit, the Comstock Lode on the eastern side of the Sierra Nevada. Huge mansions and hotels rose in fashionable neighborhoods on the hills above the bay.

Immigrants Came and Stayed

Fortune seekers from around the world heard the call—Italians, South Americans, Chinese, even Russians and Pacific Islanders. In the small valleys and on the nearly thirty-six hills of the city, ethnic neighborhoods grew up, each with their own tastes and traditions. Sicilian fishers settled in North Beach. The Chinese, who built the transcontinental railroads, lived near the docks.

In a sunny valley that seems to escape the city's famous fog, the Mission District has always been home to immigrants. Street names—Valencia, Guerrero, Dolores, and Sanchez—recall the Spanish, who founded Mission Dolores here in an Ohlone Indian village in 1776. The Spanish were followed by Mexicans and Irish, then Central and South Americans, and in the twentieth century, by Southeast Asians. Today, half of the residents of the Mission District are Hispanic and half are Asian, as evidenced in a blizzard of small restaurants and shops where only Spanish, Korean, Thai, Chinese, or Vietnamese is spoken. For *menudo* or *satay*, *pho* or *churros*, this is the place.

Below Russian Hill, once called "Little Italy," North Beach is a profusion of family-style Italian *ristorantes* and bakeries, bars and coffeehouses, where waiters sing opera and patrons play pinball and pool. Beneath the Romanesque towers of the Church of Saints Peter and Paul, Washington Square is the outdoor meeting hall and social center, where Chinese grandpas do *tai chi*, Italian grandpas sit on park benches, and artists set up their easels.

Not an ethnic neighborhood, but perhaps a tribal community, the Castro District flies the rainbow flag from renovated Victorian mansions. Primarily gay and lesbian residents are proud of the undeniable *joie de vivre* that characterizes the gay life in San Francisco. Window shopping turns up some of the finest apparel and home accessories in the city, along with erotic dolls and X-rated greeting cards. A Castro institution, Cliff's Variety sells plumbing supplies, hammers and nails, feather boas and false eyelashes. The Castro is ground zero for the biggest annual event in San Francisco, the Gay Pride Day parade.

Mythical creatures that ward off evil spirits, ferocious carved dogs guard the Chinatown Gate on the city's oldest street, Grant Avenue. Beyond the gate, the twenty square blocks of Chinatown are a blizzard of neon signs, pagoda roofs, and dragon-bedecked lampposts, all in traditional Chinese colors that signify health, wealth, and good luck—blood red, gold, and jade green. Banners and flags fly from the rooftops, heralding the family associations—the *hui-kuan*—that unite Chinese with a common heritage. Large souvenir stores and antique emporiums are on Grant, while small trading companies hide in forty-one narrow, criss-crossing alleys, some still paved with cobblestones.

In Ting Shing Herb Company, a small, fragrant shop opened in 1853, an herbalist scurries from drawer to drawer, scooping powders, roots, and mysterious bits of dried plants onto pieces of Chinese newspaper, which he twists into packages for his customers.

Seen from Mount Tamalpais, San Francisco floats like a mirage in the bay.

Chinatown Traditions

Wearing tiny, black slippers and fancy silk pajama-style outfits, two little girls with calm eyes and shining, dark hair stand on a boardwalk over a muddy street, beside their father, who is resplendent in the full, embroidered regalia of a Chinatown merchant of the early twentieth century. One of many photographs on the walls of San Francisco's North Beach Museum, this haunting image offers a glimpse into early life in Chinatown.

"My father left Canton, China, at age seventeen, with a dream of earning enough money to open a grocery store, and return home," said Shirley Fong-Torres. "Selected by relatives as his bride, at age eighteen, my mother joined him in America in 1940. As a child, I remember taking naps in the rice room, a closet in my family's restaurant where one-hundred-pound bags of rice were stored. We came to Chinatown occasionally, especially for Chinese banquets and to see Chinese movies."

Fong-Torres, proprietor of Wok Wiz Tours, specializes in "insider" walking tours and cooking programs, including the popular tour called "I Can't Believe I Ate My Way Through Chinatown." She said, "Visitors want to hear about my family's immigration story and how the Chinese adjusted to life here. And they are very curious about Chinatown's side streets and alleyways, the herbal shops and the temples. The most common question I get is, 'When do we eat?' so we head for my favorite restaurants and talk about foods that relate to Chinese tradition."

A peek into Chinese groceries and a meal in a noodle shop or a *dim sum* joint are musts for every visitor. The bins of open-air grocery stores are piled high with dried mushrooms and noodles, thousand-year-old eggs, and bittermelons. Duck feet and whole roast suckling pigs with shiny, crackling skin hang in the windows. There are pyramids of tangerines with leaves attached, symbols of friendship, and oranges and pomelos for prosperity.

The best time to visit Chinatown is during Lunar New Year celebrations, when shops and sidewalk stands are bright with the traditional symbols of good luck, wealth, and long life: vivid red "lucky money" envelopes, plum blossoms, and diamond-shaped red papers with the Chinese character for fortune. The holidays culminate in the nighttime Chinese New Year Parade, a spectacle of glowing lanterns, crashing cymbals, marching bands, booming drum troupes, long strings of popping firecrackers, and the famous fire-breathing dragons.

Shirley Fong-Torres leads "insider" walking tours through San Francisco's Chinatown.

Handcarts are pushed along, heaped with winter melons and crates of live chickens.

One of the greatest photo backdrops in the city is the Old Chinese Telephone Exchange on Washington Street, a three-tiered pagoda with green-tiled roof, flaming red trim, and lacy white screenwork. Built in 1909 to house Chinatown's telephone operators, it later became the first branch of the Bank of Canton, which was the first Chinese-owned bank in the Western Hemisphere.

At the south end of Chinatown is a dramatic juxtaposition of curved-roof temples against the glass and steel skyscrapers of the Financial District and the 853-foot-tall Transamerica Pyramid, the tallest building in town. Wrapped in gleaming white quartz, forty-eight stories narrow to a polished aluminum spire. The whole building glimmers in the morning light and seems about to blast off into space when lit up at night. In the next block, the Bank of America's dark-red marble monument to wealth and power has at its base a ponderous, black granite sculpture—dubbed "the banker's heart."

Anchoring the business district, Embarcadero Center is four interconnected high-rises with hundreds of offices, shops, and restaurants joined by footbridges and roof gardens overlooking the eastern bayfront.

THE WATERFRONT

From the palm-fringed, revitalized Embarcadero and two world-famous bridges to the crowded docks of Fisherman's Wharf, the long waterfront of the bay is the heart of San Francisco. Near the Golden Gate Bridge, Crissy Field is a former Army Air Corps airstrip restored to marshlands and dunes, a windswept vantage point from which to photograph the bridge and watch the daily parade of freighters, cruise ships, ferries, sailboats, and motor yachts in the bay.

Windsurfers launch from Crissy Field to fly in the steady winds that rush through the Golden Gate. With water temperatures around fifty degrees, currents breaking four knots, and gales as high as thirty knots, this is one of the most formidable patches of sailing water on the planet.

The complete transformation of Crissy Field in the late 1990s, from concrete parking lots and falling-down old buildings to a splendid tidal marsh, is part of the city's campaign to restore a portion of the bay's original wetlands, which have been almost completely destroyed by development. Now a lovely retreat for city dwellers, Crissy Field provides jogging and biking paths, and bird watching beside a marshy lagoon.

Three-quarters of the millions of seabirds that ply the Pacific Flyway stop to feed and breed on the shores of San Francisco, the largest estuary in the continental United States.

Presiding in grand style above the north waterfront, the Palace of Fine Arts is a remnant from the 1915 Panama Pacific International Exposition. Like a phoenix rising from the ashes, the city of San Francisco was rapidly rebuilt after the 1906 earthquake that destroyed three-quarters of the city. In 1915, she reopened her Golden Gate to the world with the fabulous exposition. The only remaining building, the gloriously rococo Palace of Fine Arts, stands in a small park in the Marina District. Designed by the famous Bay Area architect, Bernard Maybeck, the palace resembles a classical Roman temple, graced with two colonnades and a brace of shapely maidens, their faces hidden in repose. Reflected in a small lake swimming with swans, the grounds is a favorite site for wedding party photographs.

Past the historic piers of Fort Mason, Aquatic Park is a nice stretch of lawn and a quarter-mile, narrow beach, a prime site for watching rowers and robust swimmers venture out into the icy waters of the bay. Wooden buildings at the water's edge are the South End Rowing Club and the Dolphin Club, where members have lovingly maintained rowboats and sculls for over 120 years. Rain or shine every morning of the year, they meet at 6:30 A.M. for a swim in the bay.

Within the tiny harbor here is the half-moon Municipal Pier and the Maritime National Historic Park at Hyde Street Pier, America's only floating national park. Antique vessels are open for inspection, from the 1886 square-rigger *Balclutha* to tiny fishing boats; from a Gold Rush–era paddlewheel tug to a three-masted 1895 lumber schooner with one-hundred-foot beams in her hold. Kids clamber around the huge masts and the thick ropes of sailing ships, trod the decks, and linger in the perfectly restored cabins, imagining, perhaps, a treacherous Cape Horn passage or a swift run up the coast.

Beyond the Hyde Street Pier, Fisherman's Wharf once bustled with Sicilian and Genoese fishmen—the Aliotos, the Sabellas, the Castagnolas, and the Tarantinos—unloading their catches to sell on the docks. Obscuring the fishing wharves today are a throng of seafood restaurants, bearing those same Italian names. Along the sidewalks are steaming crab pots, T-shirt and souvenir stores, marine gear suppliers, and such tourist traps as the Wax Museum and Ripley's Believe It or Not Museum. A glimpse and the scent of the fishing fleet are found by walking down the alley near Jones Street to the lagoon by Scoma's Restaurant. The catches are primarily squid, sole, sea bass, cod, and halibut, with salmon, shrimp, and the fabled Dungeness crab caught seasonally. Sidewalk vendors sell "walkaway" shrimp and crab cocktails and sourdough bread bowls of clam chowder.

From Fisherman's Wharf south along the bayfront, the Embarcadero—a wide, paved path for walking, inline skating, baby-stroller pushing, and jogging—sweeps another two miles or so past dockside cafés, cruise ship and commercial piers to the Ferry Building and Pacific Bell baseball park. A flotilla of tall palms wave in the sea breezes. Victorian-style benches and outdoor sculpture are reasons to pause, and the fog seems to drift away sooner here than on the western edge of the city.

Today the Ferry Building is the place to catch a ferry to the East Bay or a streetcar for a ride up and down the Embarcadero or out to Ocean Beach. For the F- and M-lines, a fleet of fabulous vintage streetcars were purchased from the city of Milan, Italy, and restored to their colorful glory.

Inland from the Embarcadero, the formerly seedy, rather dangerous warehouse and factory district south of Market Street, known as SOMA, was reborn as an art and architecture mecca in the late 1990s. Atop the gigantic underground Moscone Convention center, Yerba Buena Gardens is a greensward with sculptures, fountains, and outdoor cafés; on its rooftop is an ice skating rink, children's educational venues, and a vintage carousel turning merrily in a glass house. The sixty-foot-wide, torrential Martin Luther King, Jr. waterfall creates a misty grotto in which visitors walk and read inspiring quotes from his speech "I Have a Dream."

Like lights on a Christmas tree, a stunning array of new buildings surrounds Yerba Buena Gardens, notably the black-and-white striped, Mario Botta–designed Museum of Modern Art; the brilliant orange Ricardo Legoretta–designed Mexican Museum; and Sony's Metreon entertainment mega-complex.

The dome of the Palace of Fine Arts anchors the waterfront below a San Francisco skyline pierced by the Transamerica Pyramid.

A vast sweep of woodlands, coastal bluffs, open fields, and beaches, the Presidio lays in the shadow of the Golden Gate Bridge.

The Presidio of San Francisco

Originally occupied by Spanish and Mexican armies, the Presidio was the treasured preserve of the United States Army until 1994, when it became part of the National Park Service. A vast sweep of woodlands, coastal bluffs, and beaches in the shadow of the Golden Gate Bridge, the magnificent park is threaded by quiet roads and paths for walking and bike riding. There is much to see, from seventeenth-century bronze cannons to Civil War barracks, pre-earthquake Victorians, adobe walls built by the Spanish, and picturesque rows of Queen Anne–style officers' homes.

Once the Old Station Hospital where soldiers recovered from disease and injury in the mid 1800s, the Presidio museum is guarded outside by artillery pieces and cannonballs. Behind the museum are "earthquake cottages," tiny dwellings with their sparse furnishings that were erected by the thousands for refugees from the great earthquake of 1906.

Secluded trails wind through a cypress, pine, and eucalyptus forest of more than 400,000 trees planted in the 1800s. A creek and a spring-fed pond are habitats for hundreds of birds.

On the west side of the park, there are World War II bunkers to explore at Baker Beach. Because of dangerous undertows, the beach is unsafe for swimming, although it is popular for sunning and shore fishing. Peregrine falcons and eagles nest in the tops of one-hundred-foot-tall evergreens on the eighteen-hole Presidio Golf Club.

The Presidio is a new kind of national park, funded in part by renting renovated buildings. In a white-shingled house with a spectacular view of San Francisco Bay, a notable tenant is the Gorbachev Foundation, founded by the former Soviet Union president to study world problems.

A landmark on the Embarcadero, the Ferry Building (right) was the tallest building in town in 1898, a 235-foot-high clock tower modeled after the Giralda Tower in Seville, Spain. Before the bridges were built, it served as headquarters for as many as 170 ferries and countless streetcars. Fireboat crews miraculously saved the tower from the 1906 fire; old photos show the spear-shaped building wreathed in smoke at the end of a ruined Market Street.

Visitors at the Maritime National Historic Park can climb aboard the 1886 square-rigger Balaclutha.

FOGBOUND

Softening the sharp silhouettes of the new architecture is the city's legendary fog, which creates an intimacy and romance unclaimed by other major American cities. When the fog is thick and the seas are gray, they seem to flow together and silently cover the city, with only the lighted tips of the Transamerica Pyramid and the Golden Gate Bridge peeking out over the moist swells.

Surrounded by the sea and the bay, San Francisco enjoys a mild marine climate and clean, smog-free air. Year-round temperatures seldom drop below forty-five degrees or rise above seventy-five. Summer mornings and evenings are often chilly, when fog creeps in through the mile-wide Golden Gate, the city's natural air-conditioner.

Weather anchor at KPIX-TV, Roberta Gonzales said, "There is a reason why we never have a marathon in July. We consider that our winter month. When just a few miles away it is hot and sunny, we are fogged in. It's typical of everything we do here that our weather is the opposite of the rest of the country. From December through March, we do get rain, and it greens up the hills beautifully, but temperatures are mild.

"The perfect day in San Francisco would be in October," she said, "when offshore winds keep the fog away and it's warm and dry, and nights are crystal clear."

Even with twenty-one miles of bayfront and a sandy stretch facing the Pacific, this is not a Califor-

nia beach town. Hot days are rare, and the pounding surf make frolicking in the ocean inadvisable, even dangerous.

The city turns west toward the Pacific at Lands End, a craggy bluff high above the entrance to San Francisco Bay. When the tide is out, the bones of wrecked ships are visible on the rocks below. The water at Ocean Beach is extremely cold and the undertow treacherous; swimming is prohibited. A warm retreat perched above the beach, the Beach Chalet presides as it has since 1925—a terra-cotta-tiled Mediterranean villa, the masterpiece of the architect Willis Polk. In the chalet's museum are vivid Depression-era murals and a scale model of Golden Gate Park. An old photo shows a day in 1863, when gentlemen in tall, black, beaver top hats, their ladies in ostrich feathers and voluminous skirts, lined up on Ocean Beach in their horse-drawn surreys.

A decade later, San Francisco's famous cable cars made their first run, and the bright yellow icons of the city are still rocking up and down Nob and Russian Hills at a sizzling nine miles per hour. Clanging bells and screeching grip-and-release brakes are part of the rip-roaring ride as tourists hang on, gawking at streets lined with "Painted Ladies"—San Francisco's fanciful Victorian houses—along the way.

By 1925, the city had a subway. By 1930, there was regular airline service between San Francisco and Los Angeles, forty million passengers a year crossed the bay on ferries, and the construction of the Golden Gate Bridge was underway.

On May 28, 1937, President Franklin D. Roosevelt pushed a telegraph key to set off bells, whistles, sirens, and foghorns, signaling the opening of a 4,200-foot-long span across the entrance to San Francisco Bay. The roadway is 220 feet above the water, and the tops of the great towers, painted "International Orange," are 746 feet above the water.

The Golden Gate Bridge is the symbol of San Francisco, a glowing red-orange sweep of cable, iron, and steel that seems to represent the open arms of a city that has welcomed immigrants, fortune seekers, and admirers for over a century and a half. The number one destination for most visitors, the suspension bridge is 1.7 miles long, extending from Fort Point in San Francisco to the Marin Headlands.

Like the rounded backs of fat dairy cows, the bare hills of the Marin Headlands are laced with footpaths

When the fog is thick and the seas are gray, they seem to flow together and silently cover the city, with only the lighted towers of the Golden Gate Bridge peeking out over the moist swells.

In the year 2000, "Play ball!" resounded for the first time in Pacific Bell Park on opening day of baseball season.

Out of the Park

"This ballpark is not the biggest, not the most expensive, not the most luxurious," said San Francisco Giants owner Peter Magowan. "Just the best. Small and cozy. Urban, brick, and steel."

Pacific Bell Park is one of the landmark icons of the city, an emerald green bauble perched right on San Francisco Bay. No other stadium in the world has such stupendous views, starting with the bay and its passing parade of sailboats, freighters, and cruise ships. Fans in every seat can watch the lights of the Bay Bridge, the golden dome of City Hall, and the Embarcadero Center skyscrapers blink on each evening.

Right-field home-run balls—307 feet down the line—often end up in the bay, whereupon an armada of small watercraft scrambles for each floating baseball. Competing with the boaters for the damp souvenirs is a pack of Portuguese water dogs, called the Baseball Aquatic Retrieval Korps (BARK), who leap from the deck of a cabin cruiser, the Good Ship Jollipup, to do what they do best.

In Willie Mays Plaza, which sports twenty-four palm trees in honor of his number, fans pay homage to the Giants' Hall of Famer at the foot of a larger than life statue of the player.

The sleek, yet timeless good looks of the intimate, 40,800-seat ball park set the tone in the South Beach district, spruced up in the late 1990s in an extraordinary revitalization of the entire south side of San Francisco. Once a grubby industrial and port area, now the sexiest new neighborhood in town, South Beach is a stylish enclave of ocean-view condominiums, brew pubs, and trendy cafés. Next to Pacific Bell Park, the South Beach Yacht Harbor boasts a new seven-hundred-boat marina, guarded by Mark di Suvero's shining red, seventy-foot-tall steel sculpture, "Sea Change," signaling a prosperous new millennium for San Francisco.

on breezy ridges overlooking the north side of the Golden Gate. History buffs climb around the spooky old military tunnels and bunkers that guarded San Francisco, from the Spanish-American War through the Cold War. Below World War II fortifications, a narrow path leads to Point Bonita Lighthouse. Built in 1855 on a bit of rock at the entrance to San Francisco Bay, the lighthouse is accessed by a swaying footbridge. The foaming surf fills the air with salt spray and a whooshing sound, creating an unforgettable few minutes for visitors who teeter between the security of the bedrock mainland and the tiny, white building, defended by Victorian gargoyles, at the end of the bridge, on the edge of the continent. On clear days, Point Reyes is visible in the north, and twenty-six miles west, the Farallon Islands can usually be seen.

A four-mile-long ribbon of sand on San Francisco's western edge, Ocean Beach is popular for walking and sunbathing—or fogbathing.

AN ISLAND SANCTUARY

The largest seabird rookery south of Alaska, the Farallones are jagged bits of granite surrounded by the waters of the Gulf of the Farallones National Marine Sanctuary. A rare phenomenon is the annual occurrence of dense phytoplankton blooming around the islands, which creates a nutrient-rich feeding range for humpback and gray whales, elephant seals and sea lions, common dolphins and northern fur seals, among other marine mammals, plus great white sharks, all of which either feed on the plankton or upon those who do. Hundreds of thousands of birds breed and nest on the Farallones, from slate-gray rhinoceros auklets to petrels and brown pelicans. Growling and purring, the tufted puffin is a noisy denizen—over a foot tall, with a pitch-black body; bright orange feet; a reddish-orange, vertically flattened bill; and a rakish white plume. Standing upright like penguins, common murres have pure white chests and necks, with black from beak to head, back, tail and feet; their name echoes their moaning, "murring" call. Birdwatchers and whale-watchers take the full-day sail offered by the Oceanic Society, based in San Francisco. From December through March, whale sightings are nearly a sure thing.

Avid protectors of their natural environment, Marinites defend their offshore waters and coastline from human development. Not in the least "stay at homes," they scrap vociferously over who gets to use the hundreds of miles of trails in the county—hikers, bikers, or horseback riders. On weekends, they turn from their stress-filled commuting on Highway 101 to relaxation on the beaches, from China Camp to Point Reyes and Angel Island.

Surrounded on three sides by the Pacific and the San Francisco Bay, nearly one-third of the county is public parks. The gem among Marin's nature preserves, Point Reyes National Seashore is an elongated triangle of beaches, lagoons and estuaries, dark forests and endless, windy headlands.

From the 2,571-foot summit of Mount Tamalpais—the "Sleeping Maiden"—are views of pristine canyons and forests, and the Marin County coastline, once the fog burns off.

Surrounded by the treacherous waters of San Francisco Bay, Alcatraz was a Federal maximum-security prison—"The Rock"— housing the notorious gangsters Al Capone, George "Machine Gun" Kelly, the "Birdman of Alcatraz," and hundreds of others. Now part of the Golden Gate National Recreation Area, it is a tourist attraction drawing more than one million visitors a year.

Island Idyll

Reached by a short ferry ride across Raccoon Strait from Tiburon, and from Pier 41 in San Francisco, Angel Island State Park offers a day of hiking, mountain biking, kayaking, or relaxing picnics on the grass, plus gull's-eye views of ships and boats in San Francisco Bay. Once a Miwok hunting ground, then a cattle ranch, a U.S. Army base, and a prisoner of war camp and immigration station, the island has a unique past.

The easy way to learn about the history and get some fresh air is to take a narrated tour in an open-air tram. Historic buildings remain from World War II, when five thousand soldiers a day were processed before leaving for the Pacific. Between 1910 and 1940, hundreds of thousands of Asians were detained here, some for many months, awaiting admission into the country.

A rainbow appears over Angel Island during a spring storm at sunset.

Hikers trod the trail along fern-bordered Redwood Creek in Muir Woods National Monument, where thousand-year-old redwoods grow, the last virgin stand in the San Francisco Bay Area.

SAUSALITO AND TIBURON

The wilds of Mount Tamalpais are worlds away, yet only a five-minute drive, from the sophisticated artists' village of Sausalito. With villas terraced across forested hillsides on the edge of San Francisco Bay, Sausalito is as warm and sunny as San Francisco can be chilly and foggy. The favored method of arrival is by ferry, with debarkation at Viña del Mar plaza, an area tasseled with tall palms and defended by stone elephants with streetlights on their heads, leftovers from San Francisco's 1915 Exposition.

Sausalito's waterfront is lined with Victorian-era houses and storefronts within the National Historic Landmark District, an inspiring home base for artists, writers, and craftspeople, who show and sell their works to over fifty thousand visitors at the annual Sausalito Art Festival in September. Daytrippers fill the art galleries, pricey boutiques, and seafood restaurants. They rent kayaks for quiet paddles, encountering curious harbor seals and a floating community of hundreds of houseboats on the north waterfront.

Facing the San Francisco skyline, Tiburon lies on the shores of Raccoon Strait, a narrow, wind-lashed channel carefully navigated by sailboats and motor yachts. Prior to the 1920s, Tiburon was a lagoon lined with houseboats, called arks. When the lagoon was filled in 1940, the arks were placed on pilings, and today they are art galleries and small shops. Below Ark Row, the China Cabin is a delightful relic from a sidewheel steamer that plied trade routes between San Francisco and the Orient in the late 1800s. The saloon was salvaged when the ship burned and is now a maritime museum of period antiques and elaborate gold-leaf ornamentation.

On opening day of yachting season in April, decorated pleasure craft cruise back and forth on the

Tiburon waterfront, while families engage in spring activities, such as kite flying and Frisbee-tossing. Locals arrive early for good seats on the deck at Sam's Anchor Cafe or grab space for a picnic blanket on the greensward to watch the blessing of the boats.

A linear park with a par course and lawns, the Tiburon Walking and Bike Path passes alongside Richardson Bay. Sandpipers bob along the tidal flats while kayaks and rowing shells glide by, and the odd harbor seal peers at the joggers and in-line skaters. Occasionally, a small whale will wander through the Golden Gate and swim in the bay for a few days.

On a high ridge above Tiburon, walking trails crisscross the Nature Conservancy Ring Mountain Preserve, where knee-high native grasses are dotted with wildflowers in the spring. Bay trees, madrones, live oaks, and buckeyes provide shade for several endangered plant species, including the Tiburon Mariposa Lily, existing nowhere else in the world. Blooming all through the spring on a stalk about two feet tall, the lily has a tan, cinnamon, and yellow bowl-shaped flower.

BEACHES AND LAGOONS

From Ring Mountain, hikers enjoy wide views of much of the Bay Area, including San Pablo Bay and China Camp State Park, a hidden jewel, where the small beach is often calm when cold winds rake the rest of Marin. Windsurfing is a big deal here from May through October, and there is a small museum and remnants of a Chinese immigrants' shrimp-fishing village of the late 1800s. In a pickleweed swamp, the salt marsh harvest mouse and the clapper rail are protected, endangered species.

Below the western slopes of Mount Tamalpais, a tropical undercurrent keeps the waters off Stinson Beach warm all year round. Consisting primarily of vacation homes and a short strip of cafés and shops, Stinson Beach is a weekend retreat for San Franciscans escaping from summer fog. Most Marin beaches are unsafe for swimming and surfing due to undertows and currents. Stinson is an exception, although the occasional shark sighting does clear the waters for a day or two at a time.

Part-time Stinson Beach residents since the late 1960s, the Arrigoni family fishes for salmon every year in their motorboat, not far offshore. Marin historian and author of *Making the Most of Marin*, Patricia Arrigoni said, "When we are out fishing, we see dol-

phins, gray whales, and many harbor seals. On our early morning walks, the seals seem to follow us along the beach. And, in fact, one of our yellow labs runs into the water and actually plays with them!

"The weather is surprisingly mild here, even in the wintertime, sometimes ten degrees warmer than inland Marin. Winter is a magical time of year, when we get huge flocks of overwintering birds, especially in the Seadrift Lagoon behind the beach, like western grebes, willets, and killdeer, and, from June to December, brown pelicans. We love to watch them, with their six-and-a-half-foot wingspans, gliding over the waves, then dive-bombing into the water."

Northwest of Bolinas on Mesa Road, the Point Reyes Bird Observatory is one of America's only full-time ornithological research stations. Visitors can watch the scientists at work, banding rufous-sided towhees, song sparrows, and other shorebirds. This is also the trailhead for the Palomarin Trail, which leads to four freshwater lakes that are lively waterfowl habitats, and to Double Point Bay, where harbor seals bask and breed. Just beyond Pelican Lake, a steep canyon trail is generously decorated by the pools and freshets of Alamere Creek, which eventually drops in spectacular style into the sea.

INVERNESS

Just a clutch of country cottages since the late 1880s, Inverness lies within the Douglas fir forest of Inverness Ridge in western Marin County, overlooking Tomales Bay. Travelers on their way to Point Reyes National Seashore stop here at the bayside cafés and the bed-and-breakfast inns. They rent kayaks for exploring the bay and launch their own fishing skiffs.

The names of lodgings reflect a romantic, "hideaway" atmosphere in West Marin—The Dancing Coyote, Sea Mist Cottage, and Sandy Cove Inn. Manka's Inverness Lodge dates to 1917, when it was a hunting lodge, and the Hotel Inverness has been operating since 1906. A replica of a sixteenth-century Tudor-style farmhouse, the Pelican Inn has a cozy, English-style pub with leaded-glass windows and a fireplace, a cozy spot on a foggy day.

Another gateway to the National Seashore, Point Reyes Station is a picturesque, tiny railroad town founded in the 1800s. Among century-old buildings, the train depot is now the post office, the old fire engine house is a community center.

Tomales Bay

Living in a vintage wooden house beside the bay, Michael Sanders sells shellfish for the Tomales Bay Oyster Company in Marshall. Since early in the twentieth century, his company and others have farmed clams, mussels, abalone, and oysters in the pure, clear waters of Tomales Bay. Tiny seed oysters are grown in synthetic bags on the shallow floor of the bay, then transferred to tanks washed with tidal waters carrying the microorganisms that nourish the shellfish.

An avid fisherman and wildlife lover, Sanders said, "It's like a zoo out here. We see foxes and raccoons, bobcats, and sometimes a mountain lion. From the windows of my house I can see an incredible variety of birds, and out fishing, I regularly see five kinds of sharks, rays, and an occasional whale. The sturgeon get up to seven feet long."

In the twelve-mile estuary on Marin County's rugged western coast, between the mainland and the Point Reyes Peninsula, the mix of fresh and salt water and a rich, eelgrass marsh supports a large population of shorebirds and waterfowl, as many as fifty thousand at a time. Anorak-clad, binocular-braced birdwatchers are a common sight along the eastern shore of the bay, especially in the winter when birds rest and feed here on their migration routes between the Arctic and South America.

Michael Sanders is an oyster salesman at Tomales Bay.

Accompanied by inquisitive harbor seals and sea otters, and rainbow-hued jellyfish pulsing near the surface, kayakers paddle the quiet bay waters, gliding past sea caves and rickety boat docks. Bat rays and leopard sharks propagate their species in the shallows. The kayakers and sailors on the bay wear wetsuits, ready for fickle weather. A warm, sunny, calm day can change in an hour with thirty- to forty-knot winds and fifty-degree water kicking up white caps.

POINT REYES NATIONAL SEASHORE

A glance at a map shows jagged double peninsulas jutting into the Pacific off the Marin County coastline. These seventy-one thousand precious acres compose the Point Reyes National Seashore, one of the greatest coastal wilderness preserves in the world, created in 1962 when President John F. Kennedy signed legislation to save the nation's dwindling undeveloped coastline for future generations.

As a protected national seashore, the bay remains largely as it was four hundred years ago, fringed with sandy beaches and mottled with deep tidepools alive with anemones, urchins, fish, crabs, leopard rays, and baby sharks. The most developed of the national seashore beaches, Drakes Beach is protected, somewhat, from prevailing north winds by mountainous dunes. The water is too cold and the riptides are too dangerous for swimming, although body surfers and boogie boarders brave the waves. There is a visitor's center here and the rustic Drakes Beach Cafe, with outdoor tables and telescopes for whale-watching, and local oysters on the menu.

Surf fishing and sunbathing are the main activities on windswept Limantour Beach on the north end of Drakes Bay. From here, Limantour Spit Trail traces the edge of a nearby estero—a five-hundred-acre tidal lagoon. The smallest North American duck, the striking black-and-white bufflehead, swims with common goldeneye ducks, their heads shiny green-black with a large round white spot beneath the eye and a dramatic black-and-white body.

On high bluffs above the Pacific Ocean, the windswept moors of Tomales Point walking trail remind some people of Scotland. The trail begins at Pierce Ranch, where white wooden frame buildings are remnants of a century-old dairy operation. Formerly

Actually a part of the submerged Pacific continental plate, Point Reyes was once attached to the Tehachapi Mountains, 350 miles to the south. Over millions of years, tectonic movement shoved it north, and it is still moving along the San Andreas Fault, which runs through Tomales Bay, down the eastern edge of the park, and into the sea. During the 1906 earthquake that devastated San Francisco, Point Reyes moved north twenty feet.

ABOVE: *At Tomales Point, Tule elk are in residence year-round. Standing five feet high at the shoulders, the bulls assemble their harems in late summer and early fall, and fight for territories, bellowing and whistling. Recovering from near extinction, due to hunting and loss of grasslands during the Gold Rush era in California, Tule elk were reintroduced into Northern California and now survive in small, protected herds.*

pastureland, the meadows around the ranch are afloat with wild irises and blue columbines March through April and yellow California poppies and lupines all summer.

The visitor's center on the east side of the seashore outfits visitors with guidebooks, trail maps, and daily postings of wildlife sightings, including whales, mountain lions, and good-sized herds of elk. Depending on the weather, the choices are easy meadow walks, a mountain climb, biking to the beach, or horseback riding and backpacking. From February through early summer, Point Reyes meadows and marine terraces are blanketed with California poppies, sky-blue lupine, pale baby-blue-eyes, Indian paintbrush, and endemic wildflowers. Often cool and foggy in the summer, spring and fall are dependably clear and warm, and midwinter days are often mild.

The most popular and the easiest walking path is the Bear Valley Trail. Nearly five miles one-way, the path wanders through native grasses—incandescent green in the winter and spring, as golden as a lion's coat in the summertime. Left by the owners of a long-gone hunting lodge, pure white fallow deer peer like ghosts from the woods.

Families with little kids linger in forest glens and play in the creeks, while hikers press on through tunnels of Douglas fir, buckeye, and moss-hung bay laurel, arriving at the end of a narrow finger of rock fifty feet above a churning sea. Enveloped in the mists of a crashing surf, one might mistake the offshore sea stacks for a fleet of Spanish sailing ships, heading up the coast to Drakes Bay.

FACING PAGE: *When the English explorer Sir Francis Drake sailed his Golden Hinde past Point Reyes and into the great curve of Drakes Bay in 1579, he knew this was a piece of the earth like no other. Pausing here for a month during his circumnavigation of the globe, he claimed the region for Queen Elizabeth I and named it Nova Albion—"New England." The land was named La Punta de los Reyes, "The Point of Kings" by subsequent European mariner Don Sebastian Viccaino in 1603.*

Chapter 4

CALIFORNIA BEACH

TOWNS

Moss Beach to Capitola

LEFT: *Tracing the coastline south from San Francisco, Highway 1 rides above rocky promontories and coves, at the foot of the dramatic Santa Cruz and San Gregorio Mountains.*

ABOVE: *Every resident of Santa Cruz County lives within walking distance of a state park or a beach.*

Tracing the California coastline south from San Francisco through San Mateo and Santa Cruz Counties, Highway 1 rides along above rocky promontories, coves, and harbors at the foot of the dramatic Santa Cruz and San Gregorio Mountains. Between Pillar Point and Año Nuevo Point, fertile marine terraces are planted with moisture-loving artichokes, strawberries, and Brussels sprouts in a rich geography where temperatures vary no more than ten degrees, summer to winter. Mornings and nights are misty, sunny days are never really hot. Ocean waters are chilly and pounding breakers are too rough for swimmers on most beaches north of Santa Cruz, where the weather and the seas turn warmer and calmer.

A honky-tonk, seaside amusement boardwalk and an elephant seal preserve are highlights along the way, plus a handful of fishing villages and Victorian towns. Not far off the highway, the California Coastal Trail wanders a hundred miles through a landscape touched by redwood groves, lighthouses, and sandy beaches, with whale-watching vantage points and campsites in abundance.

FOLLOWING THE COASTAL TRAIL

Near Moss Beach, the Coastal Trail loops through the tangled garden of an old estate into a spooky forest of Monterey cypress and along a bluff above the James V. Fitzgerald Marine Reserve, where some of the richest tide pools on the Pacific Coast are found. Low tide reveals a three-mile-long reef, wherein lives a kaleidoscope of sponges; green anemones a foot in diameter; sea stars in ochre, red, and orange; purple and red rock crabs; and fish—as many as forty species of animals might be found in one tide pool.

Continuing south, hikers emerge in the quiet burg of Moss Landing, passing by the Moss Beach Distillery Restaurant, a cozy retreat since the 1920s. Diners and imbibers lounge in deck chairs on an outdoor patio over a surf-splashed cove, and when the winds blow cold, blankets are distributed and everyone wraps up. According to local legend, in the 1920s a young married woman fell in love with the handsome piano player in the bar. She was killed in an accident, and some say her ghost—called the "Blue Lady" because she wore a blue dress—continues to look for her lover in the distillery, opening books, locking and unlocking doors, stealing women's earrings, and scaring children, who seem to have the best chance of encountering her.

Low tide reveals pools of sea life at the Fitzgerald Marine Reserve in Moss Landing.

The Victorian harbor town of Half Moon Bay is one of the oldest in the San Francisco Bay Area.

Highway 1 and the Coastal Trail continue on to Pillar Point Harbor at Princeton-by-the-Sea, where more than two hundred fishing boats and pleasure craft sail in and out. Rockfish and flounder are easy catches from the wharf, and shelling is good on the little beach west of the jetty. Unlike the tourist-oriented establishments in Half Moon Bay, a handful of harbor cafés and fish markets are where the locals gather. At the Ketch Joanne bar and restaurant, a bowl of clam chowder and a beer in a booth next to the woodstove can be a warm experience.

Due to the confluence of fresh- and saltwater in Pillar Point Marsh, nearly 20 percent of all North American bird species have been sighted here. An easy trail leads from the harbor to trails both north and south and to a good shelling beach, where sea lions serve as an audience on the offshore rocks. In the win-

tertime, the waves off Pillar Point can top fifty feet, attracting surfers from around the world.

Due to the promise of sunny weather and salt air, the twenty-mile two-lane road from Silicon Valley and San Francisco to Half Moon Bay is often bumper-to-bumper on weekends and worth the drive for the many beaches, silent redwood forests, and farm tours. A stroll through downtown turns up saloons and country stores, plus old hotels and homes, many on the National Register of Historic Places.

Besides commercial ocean fishing and tourism, the main activities in the Half Moon Bay area are flower and vegetable growing. Within huge greenhouses and in the fields around them, carnations, roses, tulips, and irises are grown for shipment all over the world. Visitors can visit the farms and buy plants and produce from nurseries such as Half Moon Bay Nursery, a rambling kingdom of orchids and ferns, thousands of geraniums, azaleas, camellias, climbing vines, and hanging baskets.

Half Moon Bay State Beach is actually three miles of four adjacent beaches connected by the Coastal Trail. The dunes are protected habitat for a flock of endangered snowy plovers. A battalion of volunteers patrols the dunes, fencing in the nests. They also warn visitors to keep their dogs away and avoid flying kites, which frightened birds mistake for hawks.

Reflecting the prosperity of high-tech Silicon Valley, which is a short drive away on the east side of the Santa Cruz Mountains, luxurious lodgings have blossomed on the San Mateo coastline. Dot-com zillionaires relive memories of summer camp at Costanoa Camp, a compound of permanent tent-cabins with canopy beds and a swank 1930s feel, all in a glorious wilderness setting. The Beach House Inn has beachfront balconies and an outdoor whirlpool spa overlooking the ocean.

The Ritz Carlton Hotel reposes on one-hundred-foot-high bluffs above the Pacific and is surrounded by the Half Moon Bay Ocean Golf Course, a traditional Scottish links–style layout. Course designer Arthur Hills kept turf to a minimum, uniting each hole with native grasses. Only eleven cypress trees grace the course, where constant sea breezes, and sometimes gales, call for the irons on rocky barrancas and bare knolls. The crashing waves create a soft curtain of sound on the short seventeenth hole, which has no fairway, simply a carry-over across a yawning crevasse complete with plunging waterfall and a green with sound effects—barking sea lions.

SOUTHERN SAN MATEO COAST

Curvaceous Highway 1 heads south out of Half Moon Bay into bare green hills, as softly folded as down comforters. Scattered on empty headlands are cows, sheep, and a few farmhouses. Colonnades of pine and eucalyptus striate the entrance to San Gregorio Valley, divided by San Gregorio Creek and Highway 84 heading east. An estuary and freshwater marsh fans out where the creek meets the sea at San Gregorio State Beach, a wide, sandy, driftwoody strand. For a small fee, those in the know gain access to what may be the country's oldest nude beach, San Gregorio Private Beach.

South of Half Moon Bay along Highway 1 are wild beaches, redwood parks, and two tiny, historic towns. In Purisma Creek Redwoods Open Space Preserve, a footpath and equestrian trails wind for a mile up Whittemore Gulch through fern grottos and redwoods

into open foothills and a steep climb to Skyline Boulevard on the ridge. Big leaf maples and alders turn red in the fall, and giant redwoods loom above carpets of delicate, pink-blossoming redwood sorrel.

Pescadero is a former mid-1800s stagecoach stop so quiet on weekdays that visitors safely walk right down the middle of the street, ogling the Western false-front buildings and steepled churches. At the end of the main street near the cemetery, an irresistible aroma wafts out of Norm's Market, where warm artichoke and garlic bread is baked all day long. Bread-lovers like to buy it "half-baked" and wrapped to take home and finish baking later.

Crowded on sunny weekends, Duarte's in Pescadero has for over fifty years been a family restaurant serving *cioppino*, seafood with a Portuguese accent, artichoke soup, abalone sandwiches, and olallieberry pie. Local ranchers belly up to the knotty pine bar.

Up the road a half mile, Phipps Ranch is a combination produce stand, plant nursery, and menagerie of exotic birds and farm animals, a place just made for kids. Among the cacophony of sounds are parrots' squawks, canaries' songs, and peacocks' trumpetings. There are fancy chickens, big fat pigs, a variety of bunnies, and antique farm equipment. Visitors pick their own strawberries, raspberries, and olallieberries and eat them at a picnic table in the middle of a flower-filled greenhouse.

Back on the coastline, tiny Bean Hollow State Beach is a special destination for rock hounds, who scavenge for semiprecious agate, jasper, serpentine, and carnelian on the pebbly shore. As much fun as they are to find, it is illegal to take the colored stones away. Lupines and white and pink dune primroses careen off the sandstone cliffs, which are an odd shade of orange and are carved into even odder, lacelike forms called tafoni. Harbor seals pose and bark on the offshore rocks. Above the beach, Bean Hollow Trail follows the bluff two miles south to Pebble Beach, crossing six bridges along the way.

Just inland from Highway 1, the Santa Cruz Mountains are crisscrossed by country roads meandering along the banks of the San Lorenzo River. The villages of Boulder Creek and Felton offer cabins in the woods, ramshackle antiques shops, and wineries specializing in cool climate, Rhone-style varietals. In Big Basin Redwoods State Park, along Opal Creek, the tallest redwoods are called the Chimney Tree, the Mother of the Forest, and the Father of the Forest. The Skyline to the Sea Trail drops eleven miles from high ridges down to Waddell Beach, a windy spot popular with windsurfers and hang gliders.

Waves crash against the coastal rocks of tiny Bean Hollow State Beach, near Pescadero.

The Butterflies of Natural Bridges

Dramatic with wave-carved sandstone formations and some of the richest tide pools on the Central Coast, Natural Bridges State Beach was named for huge rock arches, the last of which was destroyed in the Loma Prieta Earthquake of 1989. A short, wheelchair-accessible boardwalk from the beach parking lot leads through a eucalyptus forest to the California Monarch Butterfly Preserve.

Millions of the brilliant monarchs fly thousands of miles, from as far as Canada and the eastern seaboard, to escape winter cold, returning to the same groves of eucalyptus, pines, and cypress on the California coast as their ancestors did—a phenomenon occurring in only a handful of places in the world.

At their winter habitat in the trees, the butterflies crowd together into tight bundles. In numbers of up to two hundred thousand, they flutter in the sunshine as their orange-and-black wings dry each morning. In the springtime, they head north and east again, singly, not in flocks.

From early October through March at the California Monarch Butterfly Preserve, thousands of butterflies hang in pendulous bunches in the trees and move about in great golden clouds.

California's first state park, Big Basin Redwoods State Park is a cool, green warren of thousand-year-old redwood groves.

A Hostel Environment

No longer just for the young and foot-loose, hostels on the California coast are among the most beautifully located and commodious of any in the world. Most have private rooms for couples and families, and some have individual cabins and houses, in addition to traditional dormitory-style rooms.

On a dazzling promontory on the San Mateo Coast, the Pigeon Point Lighthouse Hostel is a popular one, with four vintage houses that once were homes for the lighthouse keepers and Coast Guard families. Perched within a few hundred yards of the surf, this hostel has marvelous views, tide pools, breezy walking trails, and the extravagance of an outdoor hot tub within sight and sound of crashing waves and passing whales.

A good reason to try hostels is the chance to meet adventurous people from all over the world; hostelers tend to be an outdoorsy, international lot.

The foggy San Mateo coastline and its offshore rocks and sea stacks caused shipwrecks in the nineteenth century. Built in 1872, Pigeon Point Lighthouse was named for the Boston clipper ship Carrier Pigeon, *which went down off the point. In 1896, the* Columbia *ran aground and the residents of nearby Pescadero scavenged barrels of white paint from the wreckage, using it to paint the entire town, which today continues the tradition of white houses.*

High above the curls of "Steamers Lane," the Santa Cruz Surfing Museum at Mark Abbott Memorial Lighthouse exhibits a hundred years of surfing history, including the famous "Shark Attack" surfboard.

FUN AT THE BEACH BOARDWALK

Out of the fog belt at the top of Monterey Bay, the town of Santa Cruz is fringed with twenty miles of sandy beaches and an old-fashioned waterfront amusement park. The climate is mild and the surf's up every month of the year. Rebuilt and restored completely since a major earthquake in 1989, the town comprises architecturally significant homes, from Queen Anne, Gothic Revival, and Mission Revival mansions to California Craftsman bungalows. The main street—called the Pacific Garden Mall—is a tree-shaded boulevard of more than two hundred boutiques, art galleries, and outdoor cafés, where musical performances and festivals take place in the summer. The attitude is young and creative, due to a large population of University of California at Santa Cruz students and a contingent of artists and musicians. Sidewalk sculptures and building-size murals reflect a strong emphasis on the arts.

Down at the waterfront, the tame waters off Cowell Beach make this the best Santa Cruz beach for beginning surfers and swimmers. As if in a child's dream of summer vacation, the Santa Cruz Beach Boardwalk smells of cotton candy and caramel corn. Strings of carnival lights illuminate the faces of families crowded around pool tables, air hockey, a shooting gallery, mini-golf, and bumper cars. Live bands play Golden Oldie hits on summer nights.

Across from the boardwalk on the Santa Cruz Wharf, souvenir shops line up for tourists' dollars. Fresh seafood is on sale in the fish markets and restaurants, and some people try fishing and crabbing off the pier, vying with the resident sea lions for a catch. A lively array of fishing boats, sailing yachts, kayaks, and bay cruisers add to the postcard view.

Although Santa Cruz waters are chilly, compared to Southern California, and reefs and beach breaks create dynamic wave structures at Steamers Lane and at Pleasure Point, where the surfing subculture convenes at board shops and coffeehouses. Windsurfers favor Twin Lakes State Beach, cleaved by a small-craft harbor and Schwan Lagoon, a sanctuary for Virginia rails, chickadees, and belted kingfishers. Within the sandstone cliffs backing Seacliff State Beach are the fossilized remains of multimillion-year-old sea creatures. Above the two-mile shoreline, a paved pathway overlooks a five-hundred-foot wooden pier and the wreck of a concrete ship, both roosting spots for sea birds and for fishermen.

A cool, green retreat in the highlands of Santa Cruz, the Forest of Nisene Marks State Park is a densely forested, lightly developed wilderness. In elevations from 100 to 2,600 feet, Aptos Creek is rimmed with willows and ferns. Clear cut at the turn of the twentieth century, the forest is primarily second-growth redwoods. Silver salmon and steelhead fishing is good in the creek, which is joined by Bridge Creek and ends up in Monterey Bay.

From the Santa Cruz waterfront north, West Cliff Drive winds along the ocean bluffs and is popular for walking and biking.

ABOVE: *The Santa Cruz Beach Boardwalk is the only beachside amusement park on the West Coast.*

RIGHT: *Son of the famous American carousel builder, Charles Looff, Santa Cruz resident Arthur Looff built the Giant Dipper, the roller coaster at the Santa Cruz Beach Boardwalk, in 1924. He envisioned it as a "combination earthquake, balloon ascension and aeroplane drop." With speeds up to fifty-five miles per hour on thrilling dips and curves, it's still a rip-roaring ride.*

Elephants on Parade

Sailing along the central California coast in January 1603, in the service of the Spanish king, the explorer Don Sebastian Vizcaino spotted a rocky promontory and named it Punta del Año Nuevo—New Year's Point. If he had actually landed here, he may well have heard the primal bellows of elephant seals filling the air.

Looking much as they did four hundred years ago, the grassy dunes below Point Año Nuevo are where the largest groups of northern elephant seals in the world come to breed, from December through March. Seeing the elephant seals for many people is the highlight of a trip down Highway 1 on the California coast.

Protected within Año Nuevo State Reserve in San Mateo County, as many as 2,500 seals spend their honeymoons here, breeding, giving birth, and molting. Bull males can be as long as seventeen feet and weigh three thousand pounds, with females about two-thirds the length and weight. Grunting and lounging around on the beach, a bull will slam up against other males in brief, violent battles for dominance, throw his huge head back—his distinctive proboscis and blubbered body flapping and shuddering—and sink his teeth into the necks of his opponents.

During the breeding season, visitors are required to take guided tours for their own protection. Other months, when the seals come and go in smaller numbers and in cheerier states of mind, trails and a boardwalk through the dunes are open.

Elephant seals were hunted for oil in the nineteenth century and by 1869 were considered extinct. In 1892, a few of the animals were sighted on an island off Baja California. Protected to some extent by the Mexican government, they eventually showed up again at Año Nuevo in the 1960s and now number about sixty thousand in twelve colonies on the Pacific coast.

A Village by the Sea

Just south of Santa Cruz, Capitola lies at the edge of a small, protected beach where Soquel Creek, a tributary of the Soquel River, enters the Pacific. A quaint art colony welcoming vacationers since 1861, Capitola is wall-to-wall souvenir stores and art galleries. Between high cliffs, Capitola Beach sports a scruffy fishing pier and cafés with waterfront decks.

An only-in-Capitola event, the annual National Begonia Festival features a parade of begonia-bedecked barges that float down Soquel Creek, bringing locals and college students together for days of work and fun.

"Everyone meets at 5:30 A.M. and trucks down to the begonia fields in Salinas, where we spend the morning in the fields, picking huge red, orange, yellow, and white begonia blossoms and bring them back to the creekside, where the flowering of the wood frames begins," said Jessica Misuraca, a former student at the University of California at Santa Cruz. "Our fingers turn black, wiring the flowers for hours.

"We work all day and most of the night, rising early on parade day to finish the float. Finally, three guys crawl inside the float, and three or four 'frogmen,' who wear wetsuits, jump into the stream and guide our float in line with the others."

A huge crowd gathers along the riverbanks and on Capitola Bridge. They come in rowboats, paddleboats, and canoes to watch the parade proceed down the river, under the bridge, and around the little lagoon to be judged. Each float team has its own music blasting through town as they rock along.

Misuraca said, "One year we created a 'Lion King' float, complete with a beautiful, golden begonia lion that moved and roared. As we neared the bridge, we realized that the lion was about a foot too tall. At first, we tried to force it through, to no avail, and then people began to jump into the river from the bridge and the shoreline, from our team and from other floats. Everyone hung onto the float, helping to weigh it down. We made it through, and made the front page of the *Santa Cruz Sentinel*."

The slate gray fog of early morning paints a luminous foreground for a compound of 1920s pink stucco apartments, standing on the Capitola waterfront like a movie stage set.

Chapter 5

Old Monterey and Big Sur

Moss Landing to Jade Cove

Left: *Spanish explorers called it El Pais Grande del Sur—"the big country to the south"—and they declined to brave the harsh topography dominated by the Santa Lucia Mountains, which lunge in thousand-foot cliffs into the sea.*

Above: *The lone cypress clings to the rocks on the Monterey Peninsula.*

Explorer Juan Rodriguez Cabrillo sailed into the great sweep of Monterey Bay in 1542, claiming the magnificent coastline for the king of Spain. Heavy seas prevented a landing, and he sailed on. It was two centuries later when Gaspar de Portola and Padre Junipero Serra and a battalion of soldiers settled in, building a mission and a presidio, and beginning a century of occupation that left an enchanting architectural heritage. Monterey's "Path of History" looks like old Spain, with gnarled old olive trees and courtyard gardens surrounding red-tile-roofed adobe houses and haciendas built by the early conquistadors.

Father Serra's mission church is the jewel of the fairy-tale village of Carmel-by-the-Sea, where stone cottages hide in the cypress trees above Carmel Bay. Modern adventurers play golf at Pebble Beach on some of the world's most acclaimed courses. Hikers and bikers head for the Monterey Peninsula Recreational Trail, while scuba divers and kayakers discover marine wildlife in Monterey Bay. Nature lovers visit Point Lobos State Reserve to see the dramatic headlands and coves described by Robert Louis Stevenson as "the most beautiful meeting of land and sea on earth."

In stark contrast to the busy, vacation towns of Monterey and Carmel is the wild beauty of the Big Sur coast, a misty mountain kingdom fringed with craggy beaches that sparkle with waterfalls.

Early California lives on the "Path of History" in Monterey State Historic Park.

OLD TOWN MONTEREY

In the oldest part of Monterey, museums cluster in a pleasant, gardenlike network of streets on the Monterey State Historic Park "Path of History," where two hundred years of Spanish, Mexican, Native American, and early California history is made real. Children love Colton Hall, a century-old school on a grassy knoll, with little wooden desks and tintypes of the pupils from days gone by. Behind the school and around this part of town are small adobes, some of the first homes built in California.

The long seagoing life of Monterey is chronicled at the Maritime Museum of Monterey at Fisherman's Wharf. Built in 1846, the original wharf was headquarters for whalers and trading vessels bringing goods from around Cape Horn and for the huge harvests of the sardine industry. Across the way, the Custom House is California's oldest public building, where the twenty-eight-star American flag was raised in 1846, claiming vast western territory for the United States.

Chock-a-block with seafood restaurants and souvenir shops, today's Fisherman's Wharf is delightfully weatherworn and smells of salt spray and caramel corn. On a second, newer wharf, the commercial fishing fleet unloads a daily catch of salmon, albacore, and squid, bound for the gourmet restaurants of the Monterey Peninsula and the San Francisco Bay Area.

Once a few blocks of dilapidated cannery buildings inhabited by ghosts from John Steinbeck's stories, the waterfront promenade of Cannery Row is now rampant with antiques shops and fancy hotels, art galleries and seafood cafés, a wax museum and a winery. In 1945, this was the fishing capital of the world, where Italian fishers brought in a quarter-million tons of sardines a year, spending their pay in honky-tonk bars and bordellos on the noisy, smelly boardwalks. A large population of Asians worked in the canneries and set up small groceries. Lee Chong's Heavenly Flower Grocery—once a grocery, a bank, and a gambling hall—is now an antiques shop. In the 1940s, as the sardines disappeared and the canneries closed, Steinbeck remembered the old Cannery Row as "a poem, a stink, a grating noise, a quality of life, a tone, a habit, a nostalgia, a dream."

Restored smokestacks and boilers on a behemoth of a building create a cross between an old sardine cannery and a contemporary architectural masterpiece—the Monterey Bay Aquarium, one of the most popular attractions in California, with nearly two million visitors a year. Peering through immense windows into Monterey Bay habitats, visitors feel immersed in the watery worlds of sharks, eels, dolphins, rays, and

The Birds of Elkhorn Slough

Birdwatchers paddle the waters of Elkhorn Slough.

The "peep" of summer, the diminutive sanderling runs tirelessly before the surf, searching for small invertebrates washed up on the shore. Not the least bit shy, he probes with his stiletto-like beak for food in the mudflats of Elkhorn Slough while humans peer at him through binoculars. Located near Moss Landing, the Elkhorn Slough National Estuarine Research Reserve is prime feeding and resting territory for the sanderling, which annually flies from nesting grounds in Arctic Canada to Chile and back.

Of the three hundred thousand acres of salt and freshwater marshes, lagoons and fens that once existed on California's coast, this pristine slough on Monterey Bay is part of the barely seventy thousand acres of wetlands remaining, a precious sanctuary for migrating birds and a nursery for sea creatures. The wildlife seems oblivious of the kayakers who ply the waterways and hikers who trod five miles of trails among marsh grasses and reeds. Uttering a loud *kraak* when startled, great blue herons will rise as if in slow motion, their fifty-inch wingspans propelling them lazily aloft.

A California record was set here for the most species of birds seen in a day, more than 260, including endangered snowy plovers, golden eagles, clapper rails, brown pelicans, least terns, and dozens more types of wading and flying birds and ducks. Leopard sharks and bat rays are born in the shallows, while harbor seals bask on the mud and protect their young from the predators of the open ocean.

Operated by nine California state universities, Moss Landing Marine Laboratory conducts natural history walking tours of the slough, and Slough Safari takes sightseers on narrated kayak and pontoon-boat tours.

On the rocks at the edge of Monterey Bay, the outdoor terrace of the Monterey Bay Aquarium is a sunny vantage point for a lively passing scene of watercraft, from scuba divers' rafts to motor yachts, sailboats, kayaks, and the bobbing heads of sea otters and harbor seals.

At the Monterey Bay Aquarium, visitors peer into the three-story Kelp Forest.

Window on the Sea

Stepping into the Outer Bay exhibit at the Monterey Bay Aquarium feels like descending beneath the surface of Monterey Bay. Blue light flickers across the walls and floor. A silver rain of anchovies shimmers overhead. A solid wall of gleaming, heavyweight bluefin tuna glides by, enough for a thousand sandwiches. Green sea turtles as big as dining room tables swim as easily as the sharks. Dark shadows of humans move in front of the glowing, backlit window, the largest aquarium window ever created—fifty-four feet long, fifteen feet tall, thirteen inches thick, and weighing seventy-eight thousand pounds. Excitement mounts when scuba-geared divers enter the tank to feed the animals. Ten feet high and weighing over a ton, fat, oval, pelagic sunfish gather for their twice-daily meals.

The three-story Kelp Forest is the world's tallest aquarium exhibit, so immense it seems to surround viewers in a whirl of leopard sharks, brightly colored nudibranchs, eels, anemones, and orange garibaldi. Playful sea otters and bat rays have their own glassed-in homes, with very popular feeding times.

Originally in a temporary exhibit called the "Planet of the Jellies," the jellyfish caused such an increase in visitors that a permanent collection, the largest in the world, was created in the Drifters Gallery. Visitors are transfixed before pulsing, rainbow-hued beings while eerie, outer-space music fills the room. Opaque, white jellyfish gather together in a cloud, moving as one. Vividly striped, royal purple jellies undulate in slow motion in gentle currents that constantly move them toward the center, thus shielding them from the hard surface of the glass walls. The Lion's Manes are the blockbusters, up to eight inches wide with over a hundred stringlike, stinging tentacles, luminescent yellow-orange and reddish-orange, tissue-paper-like, surging bells of light.

The natural habitat of the more than thirty thousand sea creatures, this facility represents one of the most bio-diverse ecosystems in the world—the Monterey Bay National Marine Sanctuary. It is the first major aquarium to focus on the marine life of a single region.

ABOVE: *The Monterey Peninsula Recreational Trail connects greenbelts and parks along the southern curve of Monterey Bay.*

LEFT: *At Asilomar Beach, on the outermost rim of the Monterey Peninsula, the surf turns silver in the waning moon of a summer dawn.*

thousands more animals in the largest aquarium exhibits ever constructed.

BAYSIDE MONTEREY

Near the aquarium, sightseers board whale-watching tour boats and rent kayaks. Bicyclers cruise the southern curve of the bay on the Monterey Peninsula Recreational Trail, part of an eighteen-mile route connecting greenbelts and parks along the coastline.

Otters provide free entertainment, their bulbous, liquid eyes alert to the humans. Floating in kelp beds near the shore, they lie on their backs with flipperlike hind feet turned up, tap-tapping with small rocks on abalone, sea urchin, mussels, and other shellfish. The distinct knocking sound carries across the surface of the water, confirming that otters are one of few wild species to use tools. Hundreds of thousands of south-

Golfers on the Seventeen Mile Drive enjoy glimpses of some of the most famous and most difficult courses in the world—Pebble Beach Golf Links, the Links at Spanish Bay, and Cypress Point Golf Club.

ern sea otters once lived along the California coast. Their numbers decimated by hunters in the nineteenth century, they are now a threatened species, with about 1,600 living off the Big Sur and Monterey coasts.

Passing the oldest operating lighthouse on the West Coast, at Point Pinos, the Recreational Trail ends at a secluded, rustic conference resort designed by Julia Morgan, architect of Hearst Castle. Few tourists know that lodgings here are often available to the public, a real find at bargain prices, right on stunning Asilomar State Beach. Wide, white, and sandy, the beach is traversed by a boardwalk and a trail through the wildflowery dunes to coves and rich tidepools. Those in the know avoid the entrance fee for the Seventeen Mile Drive by walking in from Asilomar onto the Spanish Bay Recreation Trail.

PEBBLE BEACH

Tracing the ragged outer edge of the Monterey Peninsula, the Seventeen Mile Drive is one of the most picturesque esplanades in the world. It was a tourist attraction even in 1881, when horse-drawn carriages rolled through the ghostly cypresses of Del Monte Forest and wolves and elk still hid in the woods. Red lichen-painted rocks frame vista points where visitors stop, take photos, and explore the beaches and

tidepools. As if in a Japanese brush painting, the dark arms of Monterey pines and cypresses lean away from steady, offshore winds.

ART AND LEISURE

A one-square-mile village, Carmel is a magic kingdom in an oak and pine forest above a white-sand beach. On narrow, cobbled streets, peaked-roofed, stone houses crowd in against miniature castles and whimsical summer cabins built in the 1920s and 1930s, with no street numbers, mailboxes, or recreational vehicles to mar the storybook look. Exterior light bulbs are limited to twenty-five watts. Trees are registered with the city and may not be cut down. A number of massive old oaks reign supreme in the middle of streets.

In spite of the onslaught of tourists who shop, linger in cafés, and sit by fireplaces in bed and breakfast inns, Carmelites fiercely protect their town, banning tour buses on downtown streets and outlawing neon, plastic flowers, traffic lights, fast food outlets, and parking meters.

Shopping is the main event in hundreds of boutiques tucked into garden courtyards. Originally a Bohemian artists' and writers' colony that grew up when San Franciscans fled the 1906 earthquake, Carmel has nearly one hundred art galleries. A bevy of resident artists have included painter Maynard Dixon and influential photographer Edward Weston. The Weston Gallery in Carmel displays his work and is also a major source of prints and portfolios by Ansel Adams, a seminal California photographer whose images of Big Sur and Yosemite are world famous. Richard MacDonald's classical bronze sculptures are represented in town, as are George Rodrigue's ubiquitous Blue Dog paintings. A creator of vibrant, whimsical works, Howard Lamar is often seen painting in his studio on Dolores Street.

In a nightly ritual, locals and their dogs view the sunset from the sandy, natural amphitheater of Carmel Beach. A bluff-top walking trail connects to Carmel River State Beach, where waterfowl and shorebirds frequent a marshy delta fed by the Carmel River. Beachcombers wander two miles of dunes here, col-

Cerulean waters lap the crescent of Carmel Beach, where pure white dunes are framed by dark Monterey pines and cypress trees.

Carmel Valley Home

Former White House chief of staff and current director of the Panetta Institute in Monterey, Leon Panetta grew up in Carmel Valley on his family's walnut farm. He raised his own children on this very same farm and still lives there today.

"My dad, who was an Italian immigrant, started with bare land and planted walnut, olive, and fruit trees. He believed in planting only those trees that bore fruit, and they still do. I drive tractor in the orchard, and we have a new barn, and this will always be the Panetta family farm," he said.

As a youngster, Panetta avidly read John Steinbeck's novels of the Monterey County area. "My favorites were *East of Eden* and *Cannery Row*, because they were about the people who lived and worked here along the coast, and not so long ago. I found them endlessly fascinating,

and now I enjoy the new Steinbeck Museum in Salinas, a very unique, interactive place that really re-creates the rich sense of John Steinbeck's life and work. He had a way of describing the farmland, Cannery Row, and the people of the Central Coast that portrayed the struggle that is life itself and the challenges that all people have to face to make it."

As a congressman for sixteen years, and while in the White House during the Clinton administration, Panetta returned home to Carmel Valley nearly every weekend.

"I wanted my kids to grow up here, too. And I always found that coming back restored my mental capacity and my spirit," he explained. "In all my travels all over the country and the world, I have yet to see a place as beautiful as this. It has always renewed me as a human being, being able to come home to Carmel Valley."

lecting driftwood and shells. Offshore, scuba divers descend into the kelp forests of the Carmel Bay Ecological Reserve.

Mission San Carlos Borromeo del Rio Carmel is the second mission founded by Father Junipero Serra. The interior of the church is sienna, burnt umber, and gold, with soaring ceilings and star-shaped stained glass windows. A warren of thick-walled rooms hold a magnificent collection of Native American, religious, and early California artifacts.

A relic of the California mission era, Mission San Carlos Borromeo del Rio Carmel is a domed, Spanish-Moorish-style cathedral enveloped by lovely gardens, with shady colonnades and a trickling fountain.

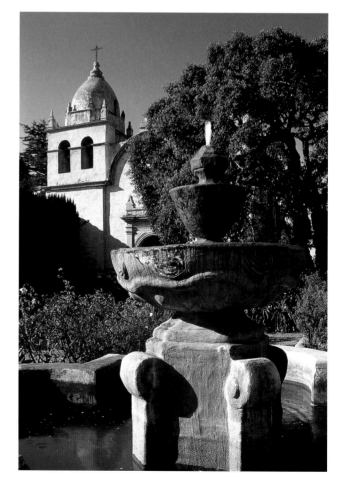

VALLEY VIEWS

The Carmel River runs between two small mountain ranges through Carmel Valley's horse farms and pastureland in a tawny climate that is warm and dry when fog blankets the coastline. Near tiny Carmel Valley Village, a dozen miles inland from Highway 1, are golf courses, a few luxurious ranch resorts, and several wineries.

Five thousand acres of wilderness are crisscrossed by hiking trails in Garland Ranch Regional Park. Skirting the Carmel River and rising to oak-covered ridges, popular paths are the Lupine Loop and the Waterfall Trail to the mesa. In spring, wildflowers explode in great colorful clouds, water rushes over the falls, and the pond on the mesa is surrounded by lush grass.

Picnic sites under the willows beside the river are pleasant in the summertime, when temperatures can reach the high nineties. John Steinbeck wrote in *Cannery Row*, "The Carmel (River) crackles among round boulders, wanders lazily under sycamores, spills into pools, drops in against banks where crayfish live . . . frogs blink from its banks and the deep ferns grow beside it. The quail call beside it and the wild doves come whistling in at dusk. It's everything a river should be."

National Marine Sanctuaries

"At eighty feet, we found the usual suspects, but we were just nibbling at the surface of the great depth of Monterey Bay," said Dr. Sylvia Earle, describing a dive in Monterey Bay. "At eight hundred feet, we found vast gardens of stars, explosions of other forms of life and new varieties of krill, so fundamental to the food chain, from rock fish to the great blue whales."

Earle is the founder of Sustainable Seas Expeditions, which conducts research on the well-being of five Pacific Coast National Marine Sanctuaries. Nicknamed the "Sturgeon General," she is former chief scientist of the National Oceanographic and Atmospheric Association (NOAA).

Earle and her fellow scientists have explored as deep as two thousand feet in Monterey Bay, in manned "Deep Worker" submersibles and unmanned robot vehicles. Believing the ocean to be the last frontier, she said, "The submerged part of the continent is less well known now than the western United States was to explorers Lewis and Clark when they set out across North America nearly two hundred years ago.

"Some people might wonder why they should be . . . interested in Monterey Bay. I suggest they look over the shoulders of the astronauts and view our world from afar. This is a blue planet, an ocean planet nearly covered with water, and the continents are islands. Contrast this with Mars, which once had oceans but now lacks what we have, the cornerstone of life support, thereby lacking the abundance of life that we take for granted, a hospitable atmosphere."

The Monterey Bay National Marine Sanctuary is one of thirteen in the National Marine Sanctuary Program and the nation's largest. It encompasses more than five thousand nautical square miles of kelp forests and rocky reefs, and a submarine fissure two miles deep, bigger in volume than the Grand Canyon.

Under siege from commercial fishing, pollution, oil spills, shipping traffic, and other forces, the tremendous kelp forests of Monterey Bay, growing up to two feet a day, provide nourishment and shelter to a variety of creatures, from bottom-dwelling sea urchins to birds and fish.

"Forests of giant and bullwhip kelp support a web of life that includes hundreds of invertebrate species, as well as sea lions, sea otters, gray whales, and birds. Now it is being harvested to feed a growing number of abalone farms," said Jean-Michel Cousteau, founder of the Ocean Futures Society. "Conservationists, some fifty thousand of whom dive and kayak in the bay each year, have observed a decline in kelp. As our population shifts to the coasts, fragile marine resources like this may not stand up to multiple use."

Along the California coast, Ocean Futures helps people make responsible decisions as they weigh the impact of human activity on the marine environment. "The (Marine) Sanctuary program balances pressures from developers, fishermen, and tourists with the desires and needs of conservationists while providing an inherent biological benefit to organisms," Cousteau said.

"[T]hese sanctuaries protect not only marine creatures but they are fundamental in protecting ourselves—we are totally linked to the health and vitality of the oceans," Earle said. "With knowing comes caring, and with caring there is hope that an ocean ethic will arise that will secure a sustainable future for ourselves and for the seas."

THE LIONS

Just south of Carmel, Point Lobos State Reserve de-
rives its name from the barking made by the sea lions
that lie about on offshore rocks. Whales, harbor seals,
otters, scuba divers, and storms of pelicans, gulls, and
cormorants are easily visible from six miles of coastline in the park. In the meadows, mule deer tiptoe
through purple needlegrass and wild lilac. The fragile
ecosystem of Point Lobos is open to only 450 visitors
at a time and is completely protected—the land and
the marine life on the beach, in the tidepools, and
underwater. In China Cove, the water can be as green
as emeralds, a stunning setting for blue-gray granite
outcroppings draped with red lichen. On steep cliffs
above the boiling surf, Monterey cypress stand like
moss-bearded druids in the fog.

WILD COAST

Beyond Point Lobos, Highway 1 runs ninety unrelent-
ingly curvy miles south to San Simeon, through a
sparsely developed coastal wilderness called Big Sur.
Until 1937, when the two-lane road was carved and
blasted into granite cliffs, Big Sur was inaccessible and
virtually unknown. Spanish explorers called it *El Pais
Grande del Sur*—"the big country to the south"—and
they declined to brave the harsh topography dominated by the Santa Lucia Mountains, which lunge in
thousand foot cliffs into the sea. Most of today's travelers venture a few miles down the road, exploring
forest trails in the state parks and searching for the
spectacular scenes they have seen in photographs.
Winters are treacherous, when rock and mud slides
and torrents of water may block the route.

Crossed by nearly thirty bridges over deep canyons and the Big and Little Sur River valleys, the road
is sprinkled liberally with vista points, where one can
take a break from white-knuckled driving and drink
in a panorama of ferocious ocean surf smashing into
natural arches and sea stacks, stony guardians of ancient shores. Making a stunning photo, the Bixby
Creek Bridge, also known as the Rainbow Bridge, is a
260-foot single-spanner.

The Big Sur River flows down from the Santa
Lucias through the Los Padres National Forest into
Andrew Molera State Park, falling into the Pacific at
a long, sandy strand. One of many hiking trails runs
along the river through a eucalyptus grove, where

*Evening light and waves roll through a cove at Point Lobos State
Reserve.*

The brooding shoulders of the Santa Lucia Mountains fall into the sea on the spectacular Big Sur coastline.

monarch butterflies overwinter, to the river mouth where sea- and shorebirds gather.

Where Highway 1 turns away from the coast for a few miles, the town of Big Sur Valley is just an unruly scattering of riverside cabin resorts and motels, a few art galleries, and campgrounds, anchored by Pfeiffer Big Sur State Park. Just south, at Julia Pfeiffer Burns State Park, an easy path along McWay Creek leads to a waterfall dropping sixty feet, the only fall in California emptying directly into the ocean. The Partington Creek Trail enters a canyon and a hundred feet of rock tunnel—said to have been carved by pirates to hide their cache—emerging at Partington Cove, where sea otters and scuba divers play in kelp beds.

About half way to San Simeon, Jade Cove is actually a string of coves, where nephrite jade is exposed on the beaches at low tide and following storms. Wave action and the tectonic movements of the submerged Pacific tectonic plate break off boulders and smaller stones from an underwater vein. The jade stones tumble in a frothy seawater and pebble bath, emerging as found treasure for beachcombers, who are allowed to take what they can hand-carry.

An exception among the handful of rustic lodgings on the Big Sur coast, the Ventana Big Sur Country Inn Resort is suspended like a mirage on a slope above the Pacific. A serene refuge for sybarites and romantics, the stone and wood compound is simple and elegant with Oriental rugs, outdoor tubs and pools, fireplaces, and telescopes for stargazing and whale-watching. Uncivilized gardens bloom with native flowers while waves of clematis and jasmine pour over balconies and tree ferns make shady hideaways. After dark, a lighted stair follows the stars to a candlelit restaurant where a stone patio floats between the Milky Way and the sea. In the middle of the night, fog drifts in thick, muffling the roar of the surf.

The dramatic coastline of Big Sur seems to inspire writers to immortal words. Henry Miller moved here in the mid-forties, and like moths to the flame, Jack Kerouac and other writers and artists followed his lead. In his book, *Big Sur and the Oranges of Hironymous Bosch*, Miller wrote of the place "where extremes meet, a region where one is always conscious of weather, of space, of grandeur, and of eloquent silence."

At low tide, the skeletons of shipwrecks are sometimes visible far below the Bixby Creek Bridge.

Chapter 6

The California Riviera

San Simeon to Santa Barbara

LEFT: *A fortuitous combination of temperate weather, dazzling white ocean beaches, and sheltering mountains makes Santa Barbara a coastal paradise.*

ABOVE: *A commercial fisherman weights his catch of crab at the Santa Barbara Harbor.*

The view from atop the eighty-foot-high tower of the Santa Barbara County Courthouse is of a vast sea of Spanish tile roofs and white stucco walls, and beyond, the blue Pacific. Like an amphitheater, the city lies on a wide slope between low foothills with palm-lined beaches as a front yard. On the far horizon, a misty island chain floats like a mirage.

At the end of the day, the sun slides into the sea, burnishing the tile rooftops red-orange and washing gold across the Santa Ynez Mountains. The mountain range runs directly east-west to the coastline, creating a sunny southern exposure and a true Mediterranean climate, a semitropical setting that earns the Santa Barbara coast the name "The California Riviera."

In only a few places on the planet does this fortuitous combination of temperate weather, dazzling white ocean beaches, and sheltering mountains occur. Mild winters and hot summers with cool nights and mornings foster the rampant growth of green chaparral on the hillsides and glorious gardens and trees all along the Central Coast.

Describing the Santa Barbara area in *Two Years Before the Mast*, Richard Henry Dana, Jr. wrote of a January day in the early 1830s, "[I]t was a beautiful day, and so warm that we had on straw hats, duck trowsers and all the summer gear; and as this was midwinter, it spoke well for the climate."

The palatial county courthouse is the ultimate example of the romanticized, almost theatrical interpretation of Colonial Spanish architecture that makes Santa Barbara one of America's most beautiful cities. Ironically, it was the destruction of most of the historic structures in 1925 that spurred residents to celebrate their Spanish and Mexican heritage. A wealthy, educated population, they restored and rebuilt the entire downtown and many private estates in elegant, flamboyant California Mission Revival and Spanish Revival styles—a cacophony of wrought-iron balconies, brightly painted ceramic tiles, fountains, archways, and whitewashed stucco. Add thousands of palms and exuberantly blooming, courtyard-enclosed gardens, and Ferdinand and Isabella might have mistaken Santa Barbara for Seville.

Completed in 1929, the county courthouse continues to be the number one tourist attraction. Fancy chandeliers hang from handpainted ceilings in cool, tiled hallways. Spiral staircases lead to carved doors, and murals depict the city's early days. In the Board of Supervisors Assembly Room, twenty-foot-high walls are covered with animated scenes of the Spanish settlement of the area, painted by a set designer for Cecil B. DeMille. A scene for concerts, weddings, and festivals, the exterior and grounds are as stunning as the interior, with sweeping lawns and palm trees, a sunken garden, bas-reliefs, fountains, and sculpture.

To walk the streets of Santa Barbara is to walk in an earlier time. Street names like Lobero, Anapamu, Carillo, and Figueroa recall a historic past. In the "Red Tile" district, a midtown area about twelve blocks long, adobes survive from the early and mid 1800s, concentrated in El Presidio de Santa Barbara State Historic Park.

Founded in 1782, the presidio was the last military outpost of the Spanish Empire in the New World, built 240 years after the first European—Portugal's Juan Rodriquez Cabrillo—set foot on the Santa Barbara coast in the service of Spain. The Spanish sailed by again in 1602, then not again until 1769, when the Franciscan padre Junipero Serra arrived with a contingent of soliders who built the presidio to defend against a perceived threat from ten thousand Chumash Indians.

The Trussell-Winchester Adobe was constructed of salvage from the sidewheel steamer *Winfield Scott*, which sank off Anacapa Island in 1853. Her captain, Horatio Trussell, combined the ridge pole from the mast, and other timber and brass scraps, with adobe bricks to build his home. Now a museum, the charming house is filled with furnishings and household items used by the Trussell and Winchester families.

The many fiestas and the equestrian traditions of the Spanish era are still celebrated with annual costume parades and pageants, dances, musical concerts, and a rodeo. Since 1924, the three-day Old Spanish Days Fiesta in August has reenacted the days of the wealthy rancheros. A *mercado* is set up in the plaza of the County Courthouse, and historic carriages and stagecoaches from the Carriage Museum make their annual appearance in the big parade, along with a horse-drawn fire truck, an antique hearse, and an old wine cask cart. Highlights of the parade are descendants of the original Spanish ranchero and land grant owners dressed in elaborate, fringed riding outfits, and ladies in ruffled gowns and Spanish shawls, all sitting high on fancy silver saddles.

In the summertime in downtown Santa Barbara, huge magnolia trees are heavy with the scent of creamy-white blooms. The blossoms of the jacaranda trees fall into lavender pools of petals beneath overarching branches, forming canopies over European-style outdoor cafés. Off State Street, the main boulevard, Spanish Colonial Revival architecture is at its most melodramatic in El Paseo, a small shopping complex built in the 1920s around the Casa de la Guerra,

In Santa Barbara is the tenth of California's twenty-one missions founded by Franciscan friars. The only one with twin bell towers, the mission also boasts a pink sandstone, Greco-Roman facade with Ionic columns.

The Santa Barbara County Courthouse is the ultimate example of the Spanish Colonial architecture that gives Santa Barbara an Old World look. Nearby streets—Lobero, Carillo, and Figueroa—recall an historic connection with Spanish settlers.

where shops and galleries are nestled within flower-filled patios and arcades.

Hundreds of rosebushes create a fragrant ocean of bloom at the foot of Mission Santa Barbara, known as the "Queen of the Missions" for its massive twin towers and commanding hilltop setting on the edge of downtown. The tenth of California's twenty-one missions founded by Franciscan friars, and the only one with twin bell towers and a pink sandstone, Greco-Roman facade and Ionic columns, the mission is a museum of architectural details of the late 1700s and of the early 1800s, when it was rebuilt after a major earthquake. On a hot summer day, visitors cool off in the dim, candlelit nave and stroll in the shade of the cloister gardens, lingering in the courtyard by a beautiful Moorish-style fountain.

THE SANTA BARBARA LOOK

Unlike most large cities in Southern California, Santa Barbara owns a certain unmistakable style and grace, primarily due to Santa Barbarans being intensely protective of their natural surroundings. In an effort to avoid "Los Angelesization," billboards are banned, as are high-rise buildings and offshore oil development within a three-mile limit.

The city has assidously built public parks, the most extravagant being Chase Palm Park, originally built in 1924 and expanded in the late 1990s. A wide, green, lushly landscaped, palm-lined strip running along Cabrillo Boulevard above the seashore, the park consists of plazas and fountains, an antique carousel, an amphitheater, picnic grounds, and a shipwreck playground, complete with a whale that spouts water onto unsuspecting kids.

Built in 1872 as a breezy site for seafood cafés and souvenir shops, Stearns Wharf remains a landmark, jutting out into the ocean at the foot of State Street. Anglers still buy bait and tackle here to try for crab and rockfish off the pier, and tourists stroll up and down, eating ice cream and fish and chips.

On both sides of the wharf, East and West Beaches are framed by a waving phalanx of palm trees, greenswards, and a paved path for biking and walking on one of the loveliest esplanades in the world. Dozens of volleyball courts crowd the sand at the end of East Beach. At the top end of West Beach, more than one thousand pleasure boats bob in the harbor.

The waters off the Santa Barbara coast are warm, calm, and sapphire blue—the same blue as a summer sky—so blue at midday as to appear as flickering light rather than a color. One of the prettiest parts of the littoral, Butterfly Beach lies at the foot of the garden district of Montecito. Seen from the beach, cypress and palm trees are dark silhouettes on the rims of high cliffs, and iceplant drops in great purple drifts to the sand. Like a 1920s flapper in a peachy-pink dress, the Art Deco–style Coral Casino Beach and Cabana Club reposes on Butterfly Beach, across the road from its mother ship, the Four Seasons Biltmore Hotel. Guests from the hotel swim slowly back and forth within marked lanes in the long pool and ride stationary bikes overhead in a glass room, facing out to sea. The plantation shutters, the sun decks, and lounge chairs are painted just a shade whiter than the powdery sand below, which is licked by a gentle sea. Dolphins like to roll over and over about fifty yards offshore. The ghostly stick figures in the distance are oil platforms beyond the three-mile boundary.

An oasis for the well-heeled, the Biltmore Hotel radiates the kind of sultry elegance that takes the breath away, causing the heart to dream of deserted islands in the South Pacific. The long arms of ancient fig trees and a brace of towering palms guard the low-slung, white stucco hostelry, built in 1921. Potted palms and orchids lend a tropical feel to the lobbies and restaurants, while on white plastered walls, ornate, gold-leaf mirrors and seventeenth-century *santos*—carved figures of the saints—are rich accents.

The glory of the hotel are the gardens, fragrant with jasmine and magnolia, gardenia and wisteria vines, and shaded by huge jacaranda, eucalyptus, and camphor trees, older than the hotel itself.

Built in 1872 as a breezy site for seafood cafes and souvenir shops, Stearns Wharf jutts out into the ocean at the foot of State Street.

The devastating earthquake that destroyed much of downtown Santa Barbara in 1925 inspired the city to re-create itself both architecturally and culturally. Locals raised money to purchase nearly the entire waterfront, which they deeded to the city. Limits were imposed on development and style, based on a perceived historical "Hispanic metaphor." The Architectural Board of Review, established in 1946, continues today to persuade developers and corporate interests to conform to a certain Spanish/Mediterranean look.

ABOVE: *Mild winters and hot summers with cool nights and mornings foster the rampant growth of trees and other greenery in Santa Barbara and all along the Central Coast.*

RIGHT: *In the tradition of Santa Barbara's Mediterranean gardens, fancy iron balconies and palm trees create tropical elegance at the Biltmore Hotel.*

*Ezekial Gil, at work in the gardens
of the Four Seasons Biltmore Hotel*

Ezekial's Gardens

Garden clubs and horticulturists from around the world make pilgrimages to the grounds of the Four Seasons Biltmore Hotel in Santa Barbara, and if they are lucky, head gardener Ezekial Gil is available to guide them around, pointing out an Australian tree fern here, a bird of paradise there, a Hong Kong orchid tree, and fifty-year-old rose varieties. The grounds of the Biltmore are famous for a year-round display of lush, subtropical flowers and trees that thrive under his care.

Maintaining the specimen trees is one of Gil's biggest challenges. "There are seven huge magnolias. One is nearly a hundred years old, with branches so heavy that they break the wall every year," he said. "The Chinese timber bamboo has been here nearly a century, too, and I have to chop it back hard every year or it wants to take over."

Pacific Ocean breezes rustle the feathery tops of thirty or so types of palms. "The rarest trees here are the Paradise, or Kentia, palms, which are slow growing . . . the classic 'parlor palms,'" he said. "The trees come from Lord Howe Island off Australia, and we are supposed to have the largest stand anywhere outside the island. The seed pods are so valuable that sometimes at night the security men have to chase away palm growers trying to make off with a few seeds. It's the Rolls-Royce of palms."

The Phoenix palms are as tall as 120 feet, and on the butterfly palm, bags of nuts hang down, a sign of good health. Highlights in the gardens are overarching camphor trees, towering eucalyptus, gnarled, old Monterey cypress, and a gigantic Moreton Bay fig. On any given day, several of the trees will be in bloom—the cape chestnut in a delicate cloud of pink; yellow and blue jacaranda; red- and neon-orange-flowering coral trees; red gum and an Australian flame tree.

The large, bell-shaped flowers of the angel's trumpet, from South America, is a striking sight at night, shining white in the moonlight, and emitting a heavy, sweet scent. A red trumpet vine and masses of bougainvillaea grow in high, ever-blooming hedges.

Gil came from Zacatecas in Mexico as a seventeen-year-old. Starting as a garden helper, he loved the work and stayed on instead of returning to Mexico. Over a period of thirteen years, he worked his way up to head gardener, a position he has held for over a decade. He normally works six days a week and said he loves coming to work every day. At the end of the day, he often walks on nearby Butterfly Beach. "This is where I like to read my flower and tree books, and just relax and get reinspired," he said. "The weather always seems to cooperate with me."

GARDEN FANCIERS

Santa Barbarans are garden lovers and avid horticulturists, particularly when it comes to tropical species, orchids, and the flora of the Mediterranean. Throughout Santa Barbara, as if in Córdoba or Marrakech, high-walled courtyards intensify the pungent scent of citrus and eucalyptus. The summer sun filters through silvery olive branches and overhanging pepper trees. Fountains splash on the patios of Spanish Revival mansions, their grounds vivid with red- and salmon-colored hibiscus hedges, ten-foot-high stalks of bird of paradise, and year-round cascades of bougainvillea. More than any other coastal community, Santa Barbara's regional identity is expressed in its gardens.

Director of horticulture at the Santa Barbara Botanic Garden, Carol Bornstein said, "There is a very long tradition of garden-making in Santa Barbara, no doubt due to both the climate and to the tremendous wealth of early Anglo settlers to the area. They had traveled extensively in Europe and were influenced by gardens of the Mediterranean basin, and they wanted to create that effect in this similar climate.

"All around town, olive trees, Italian stone pines, and Deodar cedars reflect our Mediterranean heritage. In some of the residential and public gardens, you see citrus, cork oaks, and, always, loads of palms, from European fan to Chilean, Windmill, and Canary Island date palms. The courthouse downtown has a wonderful collection of palms."

Thousands of native California plant and tree species are on view at the Botanic Garden, where five miles of walking trails meander along the banks of upper Mission Creek and through wildflower meadows and arroyos scattered with cacti, oak, and sycamore.

Orchid fanciers make their pilgrimages to the Santa Barbara Orchid Estate to see sixty thousand specimens on display; this lovely, five-acre nursery is noted for the most varieties of recognized cymbidiums in the world, and for laelia and epidendrum orchids that flourish outdoors in the mild climate.

A private sanctuary for exotic flora, open to public by reservation, Lotusland in Montecito was planted in the 1890s and expanded from the 1940s on by a flamboyant Polish opera singer, Madame Ganna Walska. Theme gardens feature unique specimens and eccentric elements such as sixteenth-century German and Viennese sculptures of dwarfs and hunchbacks. The Blue Garden is planted with blue fescue, blue atlas cedars, and blue Mexican fan palms. In the Aloe Garden, the Shell Pond is lined with irridescent abalone and South Sea Island giant clam shells. Canary Island dragon trees bleed red sap. Aromatic lotuses bloom as big as dinner plates and bunya bunya trees have ten-pound cones.

A carefully preserved landmark in Santa Barbara, the Moreton Bay Fig Tree, near the vintage railway station, is of Australian origin and was planted on July 4, 1876. The outstretched branches of the massive tree stretch more than 160 feet across, covering 21,000 square feet. It is said to be the largest specimen of *ficus macrophylla* in the country.

ARTISTS AND WRITERS

Natural beauty and dependably sunny skies have for decades lured creative types to Santa Barbara and the Central Coast. The literary critic Edmund Wilson struggled to focus on his work here in the 1920s, writing to his New York editor, "I have done nothing but read, write and swim. The weather is beautiful and all the days are exactly alike. . . . [I]f you stayed out here very long, you would probably cease to write anything, because you would cease to think—it isn't necessary out here and the natives regard it as morbid."

The natives these days comprise more than one thousand artists and writers, and they are productive, supporting a lively enclave of bookstores, art galleries, museums, libraries, and theaters. Nearly 350 artists and craftspersons gather at the annual Santa Barbara Art Walk, and every Sunday for more than three decades, artists have lined up to show and sell their works on a mile-long stretch of Cabrillo Boulevard on the waterfront.

Santa Barbara's community of famous writers includes Julia Child and William Peter Blatty. Detective novelist Kenneth Miller—whose pen name was Ross Macdonald—used Santa Barbara as a locale for his tales, calling it Santa Teresa. Continuing the tradition, local resident Sue Grafton uses the same semifictional town in her wildly popular Kinsey Milhone series of thrillers with alphabet titles.

In *A is for Alibi*, she wrote, "Santa Teresa is a Southern California town . . . artfully arranged between the Sierra Madres and the Pacific Ocean, a haven for the abject rich. . . . [T]he private homes look like magazine illustrations, the palm trees are trimmed of unsightly brown fronds and the marina is as perfect as a picture postcard with the blue-gray hills forming a backdrop and white boats bobbing in the sunlight."

Artist Hank Pitcher in his Santa Barbara studio

A Santa Barbara Artist

"I am inspired by the abundance of the semitropical flora, here, by being alive right now, in this place of magnificent plants and trees," said artist and native Santa Barbaran Hank Pitcher.

Pitcher's vibrant murals and paintings hang in public and private spaces throughout Santa Barbara. His fish and shark dioramas greet visitors to the Santa Barbara Museum of Natural History, and his large-scale contemporary landscape paintings hang in the lobby of the Northern Trust Bank and the Santa Barbara Botanic Gardens. At the Santa Barbara Inn, his misty painting from Point Conception, south down the coast, makes the hotel a frequent stop on art tours.

"The beautiful gardens and the abundance and variety of natural flora that are supported by this climate I see as metaphors for the diverse cultures and peoples from all over the world, over the centuries, who have come here and are supported by what this area has to offer," he said. "Living here, I feel a relationship to the world of nature, and to the world at large."

"Enlightened philanthropists" is what Pitcher calls the artists and other residents who organized and raised millions of dollars to purchase and protect the entire waterfront, giving it to the city in the 1920s, and who backed growth and water moratoriums later in that century. Pitcher credits them with "inventing and preserving the unique look of Santa Barbara" and saving current residents "from the over-development of other Southern California cities."

"I have the chance to study their works all over town . . . as one might study and get to know wine," he said, "and I have discovered a rich subtlety that fuels my vision."

CENTRAL COAST BEACHES

Only the locals know about Jalama Beach, north of Santa Barbara off Highway 1. Just at the south end of Vandenberg Air Force Base, Jalama is one of the least-visited beaches on the Central Coast, a mere half mile of sand with bountiful tide pools, good surfing, and a campground. A walking trail, accessible only at low tide in some areas, traces the shore south a few miles to Point Conception, the unofficial dividing line between northern and southern California. The property above the shoreline is maintained in its natural state by the Air Force Base, and the waters here are clear and alive with marine creatures, including bottle-nose dolphins and sea lions. Beachcombers occasionally come across scraps of missiles, returned to earth from Vandenberg launches.

Near the Air Force Base, Oxnard is a sleeper among more popular southern California beach towns. Fronting a quiet pleasure boat harbor, it is a launching point for Channel Islands National Park. A silhouette eleven miles offshore, Anacapa is the closest of the eight islands to the mainland, and reachable by a tour boat from Oxnard in less than an hour.

Flower and vegetable stands along the beach road—Harbor Boulevard—and in the fields surrounding Oxnard are stocked with locally grown strawberries, broccoli, corn, Valencia oranges, lemons, and flowers, proof of year-round good weather, with temperatures never dropping below freezing. The Strawberry Capital of the World, Oxnard supplies 80 percent of the world's strawberries.

One of the most unique phenomenons on the Central Coast, Guadalupe-Nipomo Dunes Preserve near Santa Maria is an immense, active sand system, a seemingly endless Sahara of tilting, whirling, shifting sand mountains. As far as the eye can see, the silken dunes undulate, sinking into deserted beaches where cormorants and harrier hawks swoop in a sky that is cloudless nearly every day. Alongside the banks of small creeks bloom blood-red poppies, pale lavender sea rocket, and sun-yellow coreopsis. Movie buffs explore Nipomo Dunes, searching for the mostly sand-covered ruins of the original movie set for the vintage film *The Ten Commandments*.

At the northern end of the Central Coast, before Highway 1 heads into the spectacular, ninety-mile stretch of Big Sur, are two beaches less frequented than most: San Simeon State Beach, with campgrounds, fishing, tide pools, and swimming; and William R. Hearst Memorial State Beach, with protected swimming, a fishing pier, and a picnic area in a eucalyptus grove. Just north, the beach at Piedras Blancas is the southernmost resting and mating site for elephant seals.

Unlike the elephant seals at the much larger Año Nuevo State Reserve in San Mateo County, the seals at Piedras Blancas are on the sandy beach quite near the highway. Visitors can watch them at close range, as long as the animals aren't disturbed.

At Guadalupe-Nipomo Dunes Preserve near Santa Maria, shrubs and wildflowers cling to the immense, active sand dunes.

THE GALAPAGOS OF NORTH AMERICA:
THE CHANNEL ISLANDS

A sixty-mile-long, east-west-lying chain off the coast between Ventura and Santa Barbara, the Channel Islands are the western end of the Santa Monica Mountains, separated from the mainland by about twenty miles of ocean.

Five of the eight islands were dedicated as a national park in 1980. Ferrying passengers to the islands from Oxnard, Santa Barbara, and Ventura in just over an hour, large, comfortable boats are perfect platforms for up-close observation of gray whales on their annual journeys to and from Alaska. Twenty-seven species of whales and porpoises spend all or part of the year near the islands, and as many as fifty whales at a time can seen without binoculars.

A thrilling sight on the boat ride are the common dolphins. The channel is often alive with hundreds of the leaping animals, who swim up to sixty miles an hour alongside and in front of ships and boats.

Often called the "Galapagos of North America," the islands are in a transition zone between the upwelling of warm waters from the tropics and cold waters from Arctic seas. Isolated and surrounded by nutrient-rich seas, the Channel Islands are home to abundant wildlife, including threatened and endangered species, and many endemics.

Ninety percent of the southern California sea lion population and 85 percent of the brown pelicans in the world nest and breed here, as do thousands of northern elephant seals and northern fur seals. A variety of shearwaters rest here on their astonishing twenty-thousand-mile migrations from Alaska to New Zealand. And this is one of only two nesting sites in the United States for the ashy stormpetrel. The blackbird-sized bird lays one white egg in the rocks, making no nest, and feeds on plankton in the surface waters.

Day visitors and campers explore the trails, from tide pools and rocky coves on the shoreline to a two-thousand-foot ridge, discovering wildflowers, breathing in the salt air and the scent of sage and wild onion, and enjoying unsurpassed sea and shore views. In the spring and early summer, the islands are blanketed in golden coreopsis, brilliant red buckwheat, and pink yarrow.

Seen from above, Anacapa Island might be the rumpled back of a sea monster as it undulates on the surface of the water.

116

On the closest island to the mainland, Anacapa, tide pools are vibrant with orange sea stars, red octopi, and blue and purple urchins. Kayakers, snorkelers, and scuba divers head for Frenchy Cove and Cathedral Cove, where fluorescent-orange garibaldi hide in waving kelp forests, which can reach one hundred feet in length and grow two feet a day in the healthy waters. Free from sediment and pollution, and protected as a National Marine Sanctuary, these waters are sparkling clear. More than one hundred sea caves and the skeletons of dozens of shipwrecks are fascinating underwater destinations for divers.

In the coves around Anacapa, sea lions hold sway. Herds lounge on the little rocky beaches or "raft up" together in the water, heads down, fins up, absorbing solar heat to regulate their body temperatures.

The largest, most diverse of the islands, Santa Cruz is twenty-four miles long and covers nearly one hundred square miles, with mountain ranges, grasslands, year-round streams, and eleven species of plants and animals found nowhere else in the world. In the valley between two rugged mountain ranges are wooded canyons and steep cliffs where wild horses hide, reminders of when Mexican vaqueros tended horses here.

Returning from an island expedition, daytrippers look south toward Bony Ridge in the Santa Monica Mountains, where bluish-gray Southern California smog often obscures all but a craggy peak, a bleak image that makes this national park all the more precious.

Mr. Hearst's Castle

A popular attraction on the Central Coast, visited by over a million visitors a year, Hearst San Simeon State Historical Monument, familiarly known as Hearst Castle, is a Mediterranean Revival palace in a stunning setting in the Santa Lucia Mountains overlooking the Pacific Ocean.

Designed by famed architect Julia Morgan and built continuously between 1919 and 1947 for the pleasure-filled life of William Randolph Hearst, a stupendously wealthy San Francisco newspaper publisher, the castle and grounds compose one of the most spectacular estates in the world, the scene of legendary Hollywood parties and weekend retreats in the 1920s and 1930s.

Priceless European art and antiques fill 165 elaborately decorated rooms—carved and gilded Spanish ceilings; Greek, Roman, and Egyptian sculptures; Renaissance paintings; and hundreds more museumlike details and furnishings. To adorn his monument to wealth and power, Hearst bought a quarter of all fine art sold in the world at that time. In the cavernous main sitting room are white marble neoclassic statues; gilded tables and chairs from the French Empire period; fifteenth- and sixteenth-century Flemish tapestries; and a Reubens tapestry.

Roman mosaics from the third century A.D. are precious insets in the main entry floor. The medieval dining room fireplace is thirty feet tall, and Catherine de Medici's wedding dowry tapestries from the fifteenth century are, perhaps, the most valuable tapestries outside of Europe.

Sprawling gardens, terraces, and pools create a tropical paradise on the mountaintop. Pomegranate and citrus trees and palms create a Mediterranean backdrop to the outdoor marble sculpture, dazzling white against the foliage, with magnificent, valley oaks above it all. Bougainvillaea cascades over the jewel-like guest houses. Voluminous rose gardens bloom most of the year.

In the Roaring Twenties, Charles Lindberg, Winston Churchill, and Cary Grant were among the film stars and notables who spent weekends at Hearst Castle, watching "talkies" in the movie theater, playing tennis, or swimming in the Roman Pool, which may be the most beautiful indoor pool ever constructed. Brilliant cerulean-colored Venetian glass and hammered gold tiles sparkle from the bottom of the vast container of crystal-clear water lit by alabaster lights topping marble columns.

In the Neptune swimming pool, surrounded by white caryatids from a Greek temple twenty-four centuries old, Greta Garbo, Clark Gable, and Mary Astor looked out over the Pacific from the mountain aerie, sipping Cosmopolitans and basking in the ephemeral glow of peace between World War I and World War II.

Montana del Oro State Park is an excellent vantage point from which to view wildlife-rich Morro Bay.

Bird Watching on Morro Bay

The California version of the Rock of Gibraltar, a craggy peak called Morro Rock looms as a dark sentinel at the mouth of Morro Bay. The seventh in a chain of fifty-million-year-old volcanic plug domes called the "Seven Sisters," Morro Rock is a sailor's landmark and a nesting site for peregrine falcons.

One of only a handful of natural coastal estuaries still existing in this country, Morro Bay and its marsh shelters thousands of birds, including more than two dozen endangered and threatened species.

Birdwatchers find this one of the richest habitats in the state, considering that more than 90 percent of California's coastal wetlands have disappeared due to development. Headquartered at the Museum of Natural History at Morro Bay State Park, the annual Winter Bird Festival attracts five hundred enthusiasts in January, when a typical "false spring" bathes Morro Bay and the Central Coast in winter warmth, the time of year when bird migrations are at their peak.

One of the largest overwintering bird sites in North America, on the Pacific Flyway migratory path from Alaska to South America, the bay is breeding grounds for the brant goose, which makes its three-thousand-mile flight from Alaska in two days.

Kayakers paddle along the edge of an eel grass and pickleweed marsh, a busy, nourishing ecosystem where salt and fresh water mix, making it a highly productive habitat for fish, amphibians, and the birds and ducks that feed on them. Snowy egrets and black-crowned night herons are among the fishing birds that stand motionless, creating a primordial look to the dark-green and reddish-colored, reedy swamp. Common loons, grebes,

and teals crowd between the dense grasses, searching for insects.

Vibrantly blue and white with a rakish topknot, belted kingfishers perch on the reeds, then dive into the shallow waters for small fish. Building no nests, they burrow a tunnel into the mud to house their eggs, regurgitating fish bones under the eggs to make a soft bed for the hatching chicks.

On the west side of the bay on narrow beaches protected from the open sea by a three-mile-long sand spit, a wide variety of shorebirds vie for food and nesting sites, among them three types of tern, including the least tern. Near extinction in the 1970s, the least tern colony here is slowly increasing. Scraping its nest into beach debris, the elegant bird looks as if painted by an artist, with matte gray wings, a sleek white body with a black strip on the head, a white flash on the forehead, and a bright yellow beak with a white tip.

Red-tailed hawks, brown pelicans, swooping osprey, and black skimmers fill the dawn and sunset skies with their cries. Great blue herons fly to and from their rookery, dozens of large nests in the eucalyptus trees in the grove near the Inn at Morro Bay, the only accommodations that directly front the bay. The dramatic courtship of the herons begins in January, when males strut and battle for their mates.

Morro Bay is best enjoyed soon after dawn when the air is cool and the birds are active in the mud flats and tidal wetlands. The flat, still waters reflect the pink morning sky, while small fishing boats take advantage of the tide as it moves slowly out. Harbor seals, sea lions, and sea otters swim close to the kayak paddlers, curious and bold.

$\mathcal{S}$URFING SOUTHERN CALIFORNIA

Malibu to Laguna Beach

LEFT: *Setting up their umbrellas on the powdery sands of Corona del Mar State Beach, sun-seekers relax in the wavering heat of a summer day.*

ABOVE: *Nowhere is the sport of beach volleyball taken more seriously than in Southern California, where permanent nets are set up on the sand and where most of the world's top players reside. A professional sport, beach volleyball is played at the Olympic Games.*

Flying into Los Angeles International Airport, Western author Larry McMurtry looked out the window of his plane as it passed over the maze of freeways and decided, by the look of the traffic flow, which route to take home. He wrote in his book *Roads*, "Where the freeways of Los Angeles are concerned, the wise man takes nothing for granted . . . any attempt to hurry would be foolish . . . even the speed of syrup is good enough."

A former Beverly Hills resident, McMurtry knows of the slow flow of the freeways that define the seventy-mile-square Los Angeles basin of melded cities, indistinguishable from one another. The Hollywood, the Santa Ana, the San Diego, the Santa Monica, and the Ventura freeways are live, writhing, heated conduits of humanity, sucking up time and energy and spirit in the daytime, yet strangely beautiful at night, a luminous Milky Way with shopping malls as constellations.

The stress- and traffic-filled life in L.A. is relieved, as it has always been, at the beach, thirty miles of wave-lapped Pacific Coast, a sandy playpen for millions of residents and visitors. And there does seem to be room on the sand for all.

Icons of the Southland, palm trees wave all along the four-lane boulevards heading west to Santa Monica, Malibu, Newport Beach, and Laguna Beach. Ocean breezes blow away the dirty air, revealing a sky perpetually blue in a warm, dry climate conducive to swimming, surfing, strolling, and sunbathing. Not since the days of the Spanish explorers or during the tidal wave of newcomers after World War II has the beach been a more precious restorative to the bodies and souls of Californians.

SUNSEEKERS ARRIVE

At the ultimate edge of the western frontier, Los Angeles was invented and flourished in a semi-arid, tropical setting in the lee of the Santa Monica Mountains. It was portrayed in 1890 railroad brochures as "the land of perpetual summer, where every month is June." Rainfall is infrequent, with most of the twelve annual inches accumulating in January and February. Temperatures hover between seventy-five and eighty-five in the summertime.

Craving sunshine and open space, midwesterners and easterners arrived in the 1880s on the Southern Pacific Railroad. Luxurious resort hotels sprung up near the train stations. In 1885, San Franciscans paid a dollar to ride south on the Santa Fe Railroad and soon after began driving down the coast in their Model Ts.

Lynne Withey's history of early American leisure travel, *Grand Tours and Cook's Tours*, recalls that at this time "California now surpassed all other parts of the country and even the famous European resorts as the sanitarium of America and the great winter resort of eastern people who desire to escape the rigors of the Atlantic Coast climate."

By 1920, one in eight Americans owned an automobile and nearly four hundred people a day came to L.A. to stay. During that era of rapid growth, an *L.A. Times* reader commented on skyscrapers and traffic congestion: "There is certainly plenty of room for this city to spread. There is nothing to stop L.A. but the ocean, and it is quite a way off."

The ocean wasn't so far off later in the 1920s when cityslickers drove out to the Venice Pier for dance marathons. The carnival atmosphere quickened when the talkies, then the movies, were born in Hollywood. There was no turning back the glamour and, according to some, the questionable virtue. In 1925, H. L. Mencken wrote in *Americana*, "Just outside pious Los Angeles is Hollywood, a colony of moving picture actors. Its morals are those of Port Said."

Precious open space in Los Angeles County, the foothills of the Santa Monica Mountains rise above a blanket of fog, melting into a luminous sea.

*The high-rise towers of downtown Los Angeles float in a dim sea of smog. A few miles away beyond the dirty haze
of a summer's sunrise, the air is clear over the Pacific Ocean.*

A History of Diversity

A vast, murky dish between the mountains and the
sea, Los Angeles is now the second largest city in
America, with a population of more than 3.5 million,
and more racially diverse than any city in the world,
save New York. The art and culture of downtown L.A.
reflect a multi-ethnic population—in Little Tokyo, in
Chinatown, and on brick-paved Olivera Street, the
city's first street, now an outpost of Mexican-style shops
and restaurants. The Union Passenger Terminal, with
its tile-roofed clock tower and arches, is a symbol of
Spanish heritage.

When California joined the union in 1890, L.A.
was an amalgam of Spaniards, Mexicans, Russians,
Europeans, Chinese, South Americans, and even Pacific Islanders. Portuguese and Italian fishermen came
at the turn of the century, and throngs of additional
Europeans came after the World Wars. In the 1970s,
Vietnamese and other Southeast Asians fled here from
the ravages of war in their home countries. Iranians
arrived after the fall of the Shah, Palestinians came in
a steady stream, and tens of thousands of people have
emigrated here from Africa. A city, a county, a state
of mind, an attitude, L.A. is a postcard of the American dream and, for many, the first stop in the United
States. Unlike the North Coast, where daily life and
enterprise are largely directed by a harsh climate and
rugged terrain, in L.A., life is defined anew, each day,
by the people themselves, still pioneers in every sense.
No one is an alien, no one is turned away, everyone
has a chance.

Not only the geological edge of the country, L.A.
is also on the cutting edge of the entertainment media and has always been the motion picture capital of
the world. At Mann's Chinese Theater, a red and gold
extravaganza opened in 1927, famous hand- and footprints of the stars are imprinted in the courtyard, and
on the Sunset Strip from Crescent Heights to Doheny
Drive, giant billboards advertise films, television programs, and music.

In this global headquarters of fantasy and illusion,
the first American theme park, Knott's Berry Farm,
sprung up among the orange groves in the 1920s, followed in 1955 by Disneyland. Now, both parks are
venerable stars in a galaxy of amusement and water
parks, sports and entertainment complexes, attracting more than forty million people every year.

123

GOING TO THE BEACH

Denied the recognizable image that defines other communities—such as Santa Barbara and San Francisco—the denizens of Southern California create their identity from scratch, a fusion society of "Homo Californii," as they are named by Jan Morris in her book *Among the Cities*.

Morris laments the loss of the clear, blue skies that once promised health and plenty in the Southland. She wrote about the "soup of air pollution that stifles the very breath of the city, the residents, their pets and their gardens." Escaping the smog, Angelenos head to Santa Monica Bay and the legendary beaches of Redondo, Hermosa, Manhattan, Malibu, Venice, and Huntington. They set up their umbrellas on the powdery sands, turn their backs on the gray-skied metropolis, and relax in the wavering heat of a summer day. Nurturer of the earth, creator of oxygen and energizing ions, the ocean repairs feelings of urban disconnectedness, promising fun in the sun.

Nowhere on the North Coast will you find a twenty-two-mile jogging and in-line skating path right on the beach, like the one in Santa Monica. And seldom found up north are ordinary people, lots of them, who look like movie stars. Everyone in L.A. may not be blond, buffed, and beautiful, but on Venice Beach and in Malibu, you might make that assumption. Southern Californians bask in the sun's rays and in their own physical perfection and heightened sense of self. They frolic like children—surfing, tossing Frisbees, and playing beach volleyball.

Just north of the Los Angeles County line at the top of the great curve of Santa Monica Bay, Malibu retains its reputation as the movie stars' retreat. Stargazers wait in vain for glimpses of their idols, who hide behind the landscaping of their beachfront houses and the high gates of their ranches in Malibu Canyon. Although constant traffic takes the fun out of a drive along the Pacific Coast Highway—the P. C. H. as locals call it—warm and inviting waters lie beyond a dense strip of development.

"Malibu tends to astonish and disappoint those who have never before seen it," wrote Joan Dideon in her book *The White Album*. "And yet its very name remains, in the imagination of people all over the world, a kind of shorthand for the easy life. I . . . will probably not again live in a place with a Chevrolet named after it."

Vehicles on the Pacific Coast Highway stream by as the sun sets golden on Santa Monica State Beach. Perpetually warm, dry weather and big waves make L.A.-area beaches a surfer's mecca.

Disappointment aside, the magic of Malibu endures, with fabulous weather and big waves. Now an architect, David Hertz surfed at Malibu with his friends nearly every day while growing up in the 1960s and 1970s.

"There was not a lot to do except surf," he said. "We hauled our ten-foot-long, heavy boards to Surfrider Beach and just south of the pier, and to Point Dume. In high school, we used to get up at two in the morning, siphon some gas and drive as far as Santa Barbara and Point Conception to surf, getting back to school by first period. In the summer, we went down to Manhattan Beach, and San Diego, and drove to Baja."

Hertz rides the waves about once a week now, often with his nine-year-old son, Colin, and seven-year-old daughter, Sophie.

"It's a great way to grow up," he added. "My kids are doing what I did, traveling up and down the coast, and learning about weather patterns, the tides and the winds."

Hertz, his wife, Stacey, and their family live in Venice, where they like the creativity of the community, in spite of the invasion of tourists and beachgoers. He said, "Venice can definitely be a circus at the beach—total craziness, but at the same time a peaceful sort of melting pot of co-existing cultures and socio-economic backgrounds. It's not gentrified, for sure. Where else would you see people with 'Venice' tattooed on their backs or their arms? That isn't something you are going to see in Beverly Hills."

A center for avant-garde art, with many galleries and outdoor murals, Venice is even more famous for the outdoor entertainment that goes on day and night on the beach boardwalk, from muscle-bound iron pumpers to clowns in Spandex on skates, from tightrope walkers to babes on bikes. Street vendors and strolling musicians keep the party going. You can get your name engraved on a grain of rice, get free tickets to television show tapings, or have your picture taken with an Elvis look-alike.

A calm respite from the high-energy beach scene is a walk on the quiet back streets of the Venice Canal Historic District, where multicolored California Craftsman cottages sit like complacent grandmas behind picket fences in their gardens. The original canals built in 1904 were topped by arched foot bridges, and gondolas plied the narrow waterways, ferrying sightseers.

About the time the Venice canals were under construction, Santa Monica's Pleasure Pier was rebuilt and boardwalks put up for miles along the beach. A phalanx of grand seaside hotels rose on Ocean Avenue on the bluffs above the shore. In Streamline Moderne Miami Beach–style, the dazzling white Shangri-La Hotel takes up a whole corner. The Georgian Hotel still shows off its turquoise blue and gold, Jazz Age Art Deco facade and an oceanview verandah where Bugsy Siegel and Fatty Arbuckle once lounged, after nights spent in the hotel's speakeasy.

Diners in the open-air restaurants watch the sun

Riding the waves is a way of life at Manhattan Beach, where surf's up every day of the year.

A wide boulevard for people-powered vehicles, the South Bay Bicycle Trail traces Santa Monica Beach, L.A.'s outdoor living room.

set over Santa Monica Pier as carnival lights blink on the spinning, nine-story-tall Ferris wheel. Originally built in 1874, the pier anchored Santa Monica as an old-fashioned beach town, until it became a slick corridor of trendy restaurants and fancy shops, from Star Wares, which sells clothes used in blockbuster movies, to Paris 1900, a chic boutique where one can buy garb from the Roaring Twenties. On the Third Street Promenade, a three-block-long linear *zócalo*, tourists watch starlets who watch themselves reflected in the store windows.

Surfin' Safari

Just north of the town of Huntington Beach, dubbed "Surf City U.S.A.," avid surfers in their vintage station wagons and minivans assemble just after sunrise in the parking lot at Bolsa Chica State Beach. In the summer, hurricanes from Mexico and storms from Australia send huge swells through the San Pedro Channel to the six-mile-long strip of sand, while in winter, big waves roll in from the North Pacific, producing dependably good "longboard" waves at high tide.

After a stack of hot cakes at the Sugar Shack Cafe, the surf gods squeeze into their black wetsuits, plunge in, and deploy about a hundred yards off shore, bobbing and floating like a flock of harbor seals. Farther out, oil platforms could be pirate ships in the morning mist.

Busy with runners and walkers most of the day, two paved paths trace the entire length of Bolsa Chica, connecting to the Santa Ana River Trail. Across the highway in a state-owned wetlands preserve, snowy egrets and great blue herons share their reedy ponds with endangered and threatened species: the Savannah sparrow, the clapper rail, least terns, and peregrine falcons. In the background, dozens of oil pumps nod up and down, up and down, a strange humanmade echo of long-legged birds probing for fish in the shallows.

Continuing the rich athletic tradition of Southern California, Huntington High School has a surfing team, and Golden West College advertises a "trailblazing, short-term" class schedule, promising students, "you'll be on the beach until Labor Day" on a campus where "vacations are longer."

College kids and tourists converge on Main Street and the Pacific Coast Highway, ground zero for the surfing subculture. The Surfing Walk of Fame leads to Jack's Surfboards, and across the street, rival Huntington Surf and Sport displays footprints and autographs of contest winners. The Shock Wave U.S. Open is one of several international competitions held here. The owner of Surf and Sport, Corky Carroll is a local hero who has taught hundreds of kids to surf since the 1950s and who still hits the waves every day.

At the Huntington Beach International Surfing Museum, a bust of legendary Hawaiian-born "Father of Surfing" Duke Kahana-moku, old surf boards, photographs, and *Beach Party* and *Gidget* movie posters chronicle the sport's history. Main Street ends up on the 1,800-foot-long Huntington Beach Pier, anchored at the end by 1940s-style Ruby's Surf City Diner.

ABOVE: *It is a rare day when the surf is calm at Zuma County Beach, a wide, sandy strand extending for miles below the brush-covered foothills of the Santa Monica Mountains.*

RIGHT: *Every day is a party alfresco on the boulevard bordering Venice City Beach. Not so much a town as a state of mind, Venice is inhabited by artists and whimsical souls.*

Toney Beach Towns

Bougainvillaea runs riot along Highway 101 on the outskirts of Laguna Beach, a sultry town of seaside villas and some of the prettiest beaches in California. Along Cliffside Drive, the walking path overlooks small coves and sandy strips with flowers blooming nearly to the shore. Gentlemen and ladies in white tend to their lawn bowling and shuffleboard, while families rest and picnic on shaded lawns in Heisler Park, above Picnic Beach and Rockpile Beach. Under the eyes of burly fellows stationed in the circa-1929 lifeguard tower, Main Beach has a playground, volleyball and basketball courts, a boardwalk, and outdoor showers, all as clean and orderly as a postcard.

Across from Rockpile Beach, the Laguna Art Museum showcases the early California school of impressionism and *plein air* painting, which the town claims began here in the early 1900s. During the Depression, artists hung their works in trees on the roadsides, hoping to appeal to passersby. Nowadays, the annual Festival of the Arts and nearly ninety galleries draw art lovers. A festival tradition for over sixty years is the spectacular Pageant of the Masters, where models stand or recline in elaborate tableaus of famous works of art. The grand finale depicts Leonardo Da Vinci's "Last Supper."

The largest work of art in town is a mural of whales and dolphins, one of nearly one hundred "Whaling Walls" painted worldwide by the flamboyant artist known as Wyland. He installed the first of his vibrant, dreamlike, building-sized underwater scenes of marine creatures in Laguna Beach in 1981. (On the ten-story-tall Long Beach Convention Center, he created the world's largest mural, a 360-degree whirl of life-sized Pacific Ocean mammals.)

Sleek, varnished yachts have tied up in front of vintage mansions in Newport Beach for a century and more. Ferries and small boats cruise merrily across Newport Bay to Balboa Island, a quaint village of Cape Cod–style cottages and seafood cafés. Daytrippers navigate about the bay in electric boats with fringed canopies and peddle along the mile-long boardwalk in six-passenger surreys. The Crab Cooker serves shrimp and scallops on paper plates, as it has since the 1950s. And for nearly as long, the Balboa Bar has been the treat of choice—vanilla ice cream dipped in chocolate and rolled in nuts or jimmies.

L.A.-area beaches are for more than just sunbathing. The coastal cliffs of Point Dume, for instance, provide a challenge for rock climbers.

At the end of the Newport Pier, the only dory fishing fleet on the West Coast has been selling its fresh catch of snapper and mackerel, early in the mornings, since 1891.

At the turn of the nineteenth century, an Italian gondolier in Newport, John Scarpa, festooned his craft with glowing Japanese lanterns to attract passengers. Other boatmen followed his lead and today the annual Christmas Boat Parade, actually a series of parades over several days, winds through the fourteen-mile harbor. A million spectators watch more than 150 extravagantly decorated boats, from three-story cruisers and racing yachts to skiffs and kayaks, with some boat owners spending tens of thousands of dollars on the trimmings and strings of lights.

Island Days

"From the beautiful Casino Ballroom overlooking Avalon Bay on Catalina Island, we bring you the music of Glenn Miller," crooned a radio announcer in 1934.

The harborfront town of Avalon looks much as it did when Miller's big band and Benny Goodman played for crowds in the seaside dance pavilion, a landmark topped by an Art Deco, Moorish-style rotunda with a red tile roof. Mermaids swim, their tresses flowing like sea grass; Indians ride charging horses; and a Spanish galleon sails across the vibrantly painted murals of the "casino," never a gambling hall but an entertainment center and movie theater. Palm trees line the streets and the harbor, and on stairways, fountains, and storefronts are Catalina's signature tiles, brightly painted with tropical birds—parrots, toucans, and macaws.

Twenty-two miles across the sea, less than an hour's ride on a jet-engine catamaran from Long Beach, the island of Santa Catalina is a world away from the frenzied congestion of the Southern California mainland. Once a refuge for Spanish smugglers, the island turned to tourism in the late 1800s when chewing gum magnate William Wrigley, Jr. built a golf course and the Saint Catherine Hotel, which is today the luxurious Inn on Mount Ida.

In 1899, you could stay in a tent cabin for $1.50. By 1919, hotels offered a room, three meals a day, and a glass bottom boat ride, all for $10. Autos have long been off-limits and there are no traffic lights. Golf carts, bikes, and touring vans are the way to go, and there is much to see in the rolling, eucalyptus- and oak-dotted hills. Eighty-six percent of the island and the surrounding water are protected nature preserves. Daytrippers and weekenders lie on the beaches and go river rafting, horseback riding, kayaking, snorkeling, and scuba diving. Wild boar, deer, bison, and the indigenous Catalina fox roam the outback.

The resident bison herd was left here from the filming of a 1924 movie, *The Vanishing American*, adapted from a book by Zane Grey. One of America's most popular Western writers, Grey spent his later years in Avalon, writing and fishing. He lived in a Hopi Indian–style home, which is now the Pueblo Hotel overlooking the half moon of Avalon Bay, where rooms are named for his books, like *Lone Star Ranger* and *Riders of the Purple*

The town of Avalon and its harbor are the romantic heart of Catalina Island.

Sage. Grey wrote of Catalina, "It is an environment that means enchantment to me. Sea and mountain! Breeze and roar of surf! A place to rest, dream, sleep. I could write here and be at peace."

A frequent diver in the protected underwater park around Catalina, Jean-Michel Cousteau, son of pioneer oceanographer Jacques Cousteau, said, "You run into whales and dolphins and friendly harbor seals, and a forest of kelp which could equate, perhaps, with what a bird would experience flying in Sequoia National Park. You literally can fly in a kelp forest, and on a sunny day, it is almost a religious experience. You find sun-fish and electric rays. It is an amazingly rich environment."

Founder of Family Camp, a summer program on the island, Cousteau said, "Catalina Island . . . is a test case for ecotourism. Young people in our program, teenagers mostly, and younger ones, enjoy the ocean. They like snorkeling and they discover an environment which most of them have never seen and never realized is so close to home. Putting a piece of kelp in a microscope to see all the creatures that live in the little piece of kelp is something that blows the minds of the kids.

"We will make them ambassadors of the environment, better people as they grow up and become decision makers."

Beneath glass-bottomed boats and the windows of the lemon-yellow Seamobile Submersible, marine creatures are on parade in Lover's Cove, from spiny lobsters and bat rays to pink scorpionfish, fluorescent-orange garibaldi, and octopi. The occasional curious sea lion presses its face against the glass.

Across from the Pueblo Hotel, the 1925 Chimes Tower tolls on the quarter hour, as visitors wash into town off the ferries. When they wash back out with the tide eight hours later, Catalina is left to its three thousand or so residents, to the buffalo, and to a few romantic souls staying in bed and breakfast inns.

The arcade games, the bumper cars, a roller-coaster and a hand-carved beauty of a Charles Looff carousel have been creating fun on the Santa Monica Pier for over a hundred years.

Heisler Park overlooks Laguna Beach, a sultry seaside town of Mediterranean-style villas and some of the prettiest beaches in California.

Bathing beauties strike a pose near Balboa Pier on the Orange County coast.

Southern California kids in the California Junior Lifeguard Program at Newport Beach.

Raucous waves launch a young surfer from his skimboard.

ABOVE: *Downtown Long Beach, as seen from Long Beach Harbor*

RIGHT: *The* Queen Mary *presides regally over Long Beach Harbor.*

The Queen of Long Beach

A maiden in 1936, she ruled the seas for over three decades, finally sailing to a permanent home on the edge of San Pedro Harbor. Looking good after all these years and several facelifts, the *Queen Mary* is the oldest cruise ship in the world and the biggest tourist attraction in Long Beach.

Her upper decks freshly painted white and her three black-and–Cunard red stacks aloft against the green hill of Lighthouse Point, the Queen's stately presence strikes a surreal note among the city's high-rises and industrial harbor. There is something sad about the sight of the grand ship that dodged submarines in the Atlantic during World War II, carried half a million American troops to Europe, and hosted potentates and presidents on sailings between New York and Southampton. Her mahogany railings still gleaming, her Art Deco–style, inlaid wood panels and etched glass intact, she struggles to maintain her dignity above a frumpy, ersatz-British mall of fast food joints and souvenir shops, welcoming thousands of gawking sightseers who pay to trod her decks. Far below in her shadow is an odd comrade, a decommissioned Russian submarine. And just offshore, strange palm-tree-topped islands are actually disguised oil wells.

Winston Churchill slept in the Queen's staterooms on a number of sailings. Greta Garbo hid behind her dark glasses in the Verandah Grill. And, after abdicating the throne of England, the Duke of Windsor and his American bride, Wallis Simpson, were treated like royalty aboard the *Queen Mary*.

A gentle way to ease out of nostalgia and down the Queen's gangplank, and confront the twenty-first century in Long Beach, is to take a water taxi—called an AquaBus—to the Long Beach Aquarium of the Pacific, where luminous, rainbow-hued creatures drift and pulse as if in outer space. Called "Phantoms of the Deep," brainless, aimless jellyfish glow in a timeless sea, mesmerizing viewers. The water taxi moves on to shopping malls, to the *Californian*—a full-scale replica of an 1849 revenue cutter and the official tallship of the state of California—and to Catalina Landing, the debarkation point for ferries to Catalina Island.

LEAVING L.A.

Lighting up the night at the entrance to Los Angeles International Airport, neon towers glimmer with the haze of exhaust. Mounted on high, curved stilts above the jet noise, L.A. Encounter is a glowing disk wherein waiters in spacesuits move between glossy tables lit by 1950s-style "lava" lamps. Redesigned by Disney Imagineering, the fantasy café is a portal to the promise of sunny skies and a good life in the West.

Chapter 8

SAN DIEGO
SUNSHINE

Oceanside to Coronado

LEFT: *The coves and beaches of La Jolla. Topped by a meandering footpath, sandstone cliffs are constantly eroding above La Jolla Cove, where warm, protected waters are legendary for their brilliant azure color and translucency.*

ABOVE: *A Los Angeles class submarine is one of dozens of U.S. Navy ships based at Loma Mar Naval Submarine Station on San Diego Bay.*

Pacifico is the Spanish word for peaceful. Warm, sunny, pacifico California days seem to melt one into another in San Diego County, and the living is easy in this semitropical climate, or so it appears. Yearly rainfall is less than ten inches and the average temperature year round is seventy degrees. People from stormier climes wonder why San Diegans bother to have weather forecasters at all.

About twelve miles north of the border with Mexico, the city of San Diego lolls on a coastal plain facing a calm bay, protected from Pacific squalls and winds by an isthmus and a curved peninsula. Sun-seekers flock to the warm waters and white sands on seventy miles of beaches, from the surfer's waves at Pacific and Mission Beaches to the jewel-like coves of La Jolla and a chain of perfect, sandy strands in the northern part of San Diego County. It is hard to imagine a place on earth as perfectly designed by nature for enjoying the seaside.

Of the myriad places to surf in California, the San Diego coast may be the most hedonistic. Days are inevitably clear, the sky is blue, and the water is calm and glassy between the surging walls of water, creating a meditative, seductive, and often addictive quality to surfing. Mission and Pacific Beaches are favorites of surfers, boogie boarders, and volleyball players. Off-limits to swimmers, Tourmaline Surfing Park has a famous "surf break" formed by uplifted submarine terraces.

Outdoor recreation and sports are part of everyday life in San Diego. Of its million residents, nearly two hundred thousand of them regularly jog, walk, bike, or in-line skate on bay- and oceanfront boardwalks and paths. Over ninety golf courses in the county make this the largest golf mecca in the West, after the Palm Springs area. Labyrinthine Mission Bay, home to more than two thousand boats, is said to be the largest aquatic sports headquarters in the world, with sheltered swimming bays, a huge swimming pool—the Plunge—and places to fish, surf, picnic, water-ski, and camp.

Downtown San Diego

In San Diego, the second most populous city in the state, the skyscraper forest and traffic glut are relieved by the quaintness of Old Town, the Victorian Gaslamp Quarter, and a generous assortment of red-tile-roofed, neo-Spanish-Colonial-style buildings, reminiscent of the city's Hispanic beginnings.

A bright red trolley runs around downtown, from shopping and theaters to the beaches of Mission Bay and to tourist attractions on the Embarcadero, a long waterfront promenade lined with sea-breezy attractions, including harbor tour boats, hundreds of pleasure craft, and a cruise ship terminal. U.S. Navy ships, sometimes including an aircraft carrier or a battleship, are open for viewing at the Broadway Pier.

Dependably clear skies are the primary reason the U.S. Navy and Marine Corps established the largest military complex in the world on the shores of San Diego Bay. A good place to get an overview of their huge installations is from Point Loma on the tip of the skinny peninsula that protects the bay. In contrast to the high-rise city center and the sprawling vacation resorts of Mission Bay, the U.S. Navy complexes are vast, gray expanses of concrete runways and industrial buildings.

A landmark on the San Diego waterfront, the Star of India (built in 1863) is said to be the oldest merchant ship still able to set sail.

A gleaming phalanx of high-rises in downtown San Diego towers over San Diego Harbor.

SPANISH AND MEXICAN HISTORY

In 1542, Spaniard Juan Rodriquez Cabrillo was the first European to sight Point Loma, the south-westernmost bit of land on the continent. His flag-ship galleon, the one-hundred-by-twenty-five-foot *San Salvador* and two caravels, with their hundreds of soldiers, sailors, and slaves, must have been impressive and terrifying to the native Indians.

The promise of gold convinced the Spanish to explore and eventually to claim the entire coastline of California. Cabrillo was searching for a river that was believed to connect the Pacific and Atlantic Oceans and was on orders from the king of Spain to claim all the land north of what is now Baja, California.

In 1769, the Spanish returned to set up house-keeping, building a military presidio and the first in a chain of Spanish missions on the El Camino Real—

the "King's Road"—which ultimately stretched four hundred miles north. Thus, San Diego became the birthplace of California.

Hispanidad—the lasting influence of the Spanish, and later the Mexicans, in the New World—is chronicled in dioramas and exhibits at Cabrillo National Monument on Point Loma. Sea winds blow ceaselessly on the green, chaparral-covered bluff, which is topped by an 1854 lighthouse.

Mexican place names are found throughout the county, and many buildings from the 1800s tie the past with the present. In Old Town State Historic Park, six blocks of structures from 1821 to 1872 are preserved in a pleasant garden setting on the site of the original Mexican pueblo. Although the streets are dusty and unpaved as they were a century ago, the park is so densely surrounded by souvenir shops and tourist cafés that history gets a little lost in commercialism.

A quiet retreat from the crowds in Old Town is La Casa de Estududillo, a two-hundred-year-old adobe hacienda enclosing a courtyard fragrant with sage, shady with pomegranate and acacia trees, and striking with agave and cherimoya cacti. The rooms are furnished according to the period of the mid 1800s, when the prominent Estududillo family raised twelve children here.

In Colorado House, an 1851 saloon and hotel that is now the Wells Fargo Museum, a bright red stagecoach bears words from an 1877 issue of the *Omaha Gazette*: "Hints for Plains Travelers: Don't grease your hair before starting or dust will stick there in sufficient quantities to make a respectable 'tater' patch. Don't swear, nor lop over on your neighbor when sleeping. Don't discuss politics or religion, nor point out places on the road where horrible murders have been committed."

Descendants from the original Spanish and Mexican families, and immigrants from Mexico who located here in recent decades, compose a large percentage of the population in San Diego County. Their annual festivals and celebrations attract thousands of spectators. In early November on *Dia de los Muertos* (Day of the Dead), shops and restaurants set up altars adorned with sugar skulls, yellow marigolds, dishes of beans, and skeletons decorated with foil and sequins—festive memorials to departed souls. At Christmastime, rooftops and sidewalks are lined with glowing *luminarias*, lighted candles inside paper bags.

Point Cabrillo Lighthouse stands on a windy promontory at Cabrillo National Monument, where Hispanic history is chronicled in the museum and visitor's center.

Charmed and inspired by The Del, L. Frank Baum wrote at least three of his Wizard of Oz tales while residing at the seaside resort for months at a time between 1904 and 1910. (He also designed the coronet-shaped chandeliers seen today in the hotel's Crown Coronet Room.)

"The Del"

At the turn of the nineteenth century, when the cross-continental railroads reached San Diego, the island of Coronado blossomed as a winter resort. Easterners came out on the Southern Pacific, a trip that took seven days. Wealthy travelers had their own private rail cars that were hitched up to trains in the east and unhitched when they reached the Hotel Del Coronado, one of the first and largest resort hotels on the Southern California coast. Opening for business in 1888, "The Del," as it was affectionately called, was a Queen Anne Revival–style fantasy topped by steep, round, red roofs, turrets, and cupolas. Its design was saucy with hand-carved gewgaws; fancy columns and banisters; and lacy, white trim around the eaves.

A well-preserved dowager today, The Del still reigns as the *grande dame* of Coronado Island, its gracious ocean-view verandah one of the grandest on the planet. Visitors climb the tall, wide, entry stairs of the rambling hotel into a cathedral-like lobby, elegant with ornate balustrades of dark, polished mahogany and featuring the original birdcage elevator. Reminiscent of the famous Longbar at the Raffles Hotel in Singapore, the forty-six-foot-long mahogany bar at The Del came around Cape Horn by ship in 1888.

Gracious she is, snooty she is not. Guests get right into a relaxed state of mind at the beach and on their lounge chairs by the swimming pools, just as they did when European royalty and American presidents were in residence. President Franklin Delano Roosevelt stayed here often, as his son lived in Coronado, and he made

his radio speech of acceptance for his fourth term from the hotel. (As it was wartime, the news services blacked out the real location, substituting "West Coast military installation.")

The Windsor Lawn is named for King Edward VIII of England, who is said to have met his life's love, Wallis Simpson, here in 1920.

Many people remember The Del from the 1958 movie *Some Like It Hot*, which was filmed here. In fabulous 1920s attire, Jack Lemmon, Tony Curtis, and Marilyn Monroe chased each other around the palmy, overdecorated lobby and rooms, while oldsters rocked in their wicker chairs on the verandah and zipped about the bay in their varnished speedboats.

Hollywood stars Mary Pickford, Charlie Chaplin, and others frolic in sepia-toned photos hung in the hotel's hallways, creating a museum of the early days. The rich and famous played croquet and tennis in their whites and posed in rattan settees in the bar, while ceiling fans slowly turned above the potted palms, a scene not unlike today.

Glowing in the sunset as she has for over a century, a well-preserved redhead from the Gilded Age of Southern California, The Del blazes in the December night with fifty thousand Christmas lights strung along her eaves and banisters. The hotel once had the largest incandescent electric plant in the world to light up her rooms with electric lights when most buildings still used gas lamps. Early guests were warned not to light the lamps with a flame.

La Jolla, the Jewel

On the north end of San Diego, La Jolla— "the jewel" in Spanish—resembles a town on the Italian Rivera, with meandering, narrow streets bright with saucer-sized golden and red hibiscus, clumps of bird of paradise and gardenia, and palms of every description. Tropical flowers are as common as wildflowers in the gardens of the wealthy, and ocean-view villas are as expansive and expensive as they must be in Portofino.

The coves and beaches of La Jolla are warm and protected, with water legendary for its color and translucency. Within the deep arm of La Jolla Cove, in the tide pools and around the coral reefs of the San Diego–La Jolla Underwater Park, the sea takes on a glimmering, cerulean hue, a radiant environment for fish, anemones, urchins, and other sea life. Snorkelers and scuba divers in just five to ten feet of water encounter eerily smiling moray eels and fluorescent orange garibaldi fish swaying among ribbonlike green sea grasses.

Mottled leopard sharks breed and raise their young in the sandy shallows off La Jolla Shores Beach. The stunning cliff-top path and the sands are crowded in the summertime. Bodysurfers brave the outer current at the point, and an annual Rough Water Swim takes place here in August.

At Windansea Beach, homeowners sit on their stone terraces sipping their cocktails, surfers catch a last golden wave, and tourists snap photos of each other, while waves build and crash dramatically around a large rock offshore.

La Jolla grew up around La Valencia Hotel, one of the first resorts built in Southern California. In 1926 when the hotel opened, La Jolla's population was about three thousand and the salmon-pink stucco, Mediterranean Revival hotel tower was one of a handful of commercial structures. Old photos in today's lobby show a row of Model T Fords on Coast Boulevard above La Jolla Bay and what is today Scripps Park Beach, a cozy curve of sand between sandstone bluffs below the hotel. The twenty-foot-tall window in the lobby has always been the ultimate Pacific outlook and sunset cocktail gathering site, where Fairbanks and Garbo, Pickford and Chaplin hobnobbed beneath the Spanish-style, heavy-beamed ceilings.

The hotel's Whaling Bar is museumlike, with scrimshaw carvings, harpoons, and the whimsical, wall-sized Wings Howard mural over the bar. In the halcyon days of the 1940s when Hollywood stars performed at the local La Jolla Playhouse, Gregory Peck, Ginger Rogers, and their buddies tippled at the bar and bunked down at the hotel, careening up and down hallways decorated with tropical-theme Art Deco wallpapers.

Following the Pearl Harbor scare, La Valencia's tower, the highest vantage point in town, was manned twenty-four hours a day with volunteers scanning for enemy aircraft.

After World War II, residential development filled the flatlands of La Jolla Shores and the slopes of Mount Soledad. Eventually the University of California built a sprawling campus on the mesa above town.

Every major attraction in La Jolla, it seems, is sited to take full advantage of the spectacular coastal setting. Standing in austere, contemporary elegance at the Pacific's edge, the Museum of Contemporary Art, designed by Robert Venturi, is flooded with light from floor-to-ceiling windows. Among serene white arches and courtyards, galleries are filled with the vividly colored works of Frida Kahlo, Diego Rivera, and other Latin and American artists.

The well-heeled denizens of La Jolla frequent the designer boutiques and the art galleries of Prospect Street, sometimes called the Rodeo Drive of San Diego County. Residents support a lively community of artists, who sell their works at the annual La Jolla Fine Arts Festival.

For La Jollans whose idyllic natural environment does not fulfill all the needs of mind and body, there is the Chopra Center for Well-Being, a jasmine-scented temple to stress relief and enlightenment founded by the charismatic pioneer of alternative medicine, Deepak Chopra, M.D. Participants attend seminars on the reversal of aging, "Enlightened Cooking," and "Enchanted Lives." They shop in the Store of Infinite Possibilities and sip restoratives in the Quantum Soup Cafe.

Another retreat from the busy beaches and even busier freeways of San Diego, Torrey Pines State Reserve, just north of La Jolla, is a universe of dramatic cliffs, coves, and gnarled pines atop gorgeous cliffs several hundred feet above the ocean. Quiet footpaths meander in groves of Torrey pines, which exist only here and on Santa Rosa Island in the Channel Islands. Torrey Pines City Beach, also known as Black's Beach, is a notorious nude beach and a favorite with students of the University of California at San Diego, located just to the east.

Beachlovers with at least some clothes on will find that a walk south on the sand from Torrey Pines State Beach has as its reward a majestic ensemble of boulders as tall as three-story buildings, hundreds of Torrey pines cascading into steep ravines, wind- and water-carved sandstone cliffs, and a very pretty stretch of sand.

The promenade above Scripps Park Beach is a favorite sunset vantage point.

Pebbly Torrey Pines State Beach is a quiet retreat from busy San Diego.

HISTORIC 101

Not far up the coast from the moneyed ambience and coves of La Jolla, small towns are linked by Old Highway 101 and a string of beautiful beaches, cleaved by four wildlife-rich lagoons. Once the only auto route between Los Angeles and San Diego, and the western terminus of cross-country Route 66, Highway 101 was bypassed in the mid 1960s by Interstate 5, and for a time the beach towns withered in popularity. Nowadays, "Historic 101" between Del Mar and Oceanside is a tourist attraction in itself, with a semi-retro, funky look to the communities that merge into continuous roadside tourism development. Daytrippers hop on and off the "Coaster," a train that runs along the oceanfront to Solana Beach, Encinitas, Carlsbad, and Oceanside.

In Oceanside, the nicest things to do are to trod the Strand from Linear Park above the ocean, along two miles of paths around the huge yacht harbor, and to explore the pier. Reachable on foot or by shuttle bus, at the end of the pier is Ruby's Diner, a 1950s-style purveyor of American comfort food such as homemade apple pie and chili.

At Beacon Street and the highway, in business since 1929 and the oldest café along the highway, Cafe 101 is hard to miss, with its building-sized mural of hot 1950s cars. Inside, a Wurlitzer-style jukebox plays Golden Oldies at night, and patrons fill up on thick milk shakes and burgers. Old photos line the walls, recalling Oceanside history. Among architectural landmarks reminiscent of the 1920s are Robert's Cottages, bright pink units of a motorcourt built in 1928. Some of the tiny houses with their miniature front porches sold for less than six-thousand dollars in the 1950s.

The north-county town with the highest level of quaintness is Carlsbad, known less for its beach than its antiques shops and European-style vintage buildings, primarily Dutch, Bohemian, and Victorian. Seafood shacks and open-air cafés are casual, with quirky names such as Shrimply Delicious, the Belly Up Tavern, and Johnny Mañanas. Above the Carlsbad beaches, a wide, paved path is favored by joggers and in-line skaters. The town beach has the alarming habit of nearly disappearing from year to year when the sand washes away.

Inland from the town of Carlsbad, on a mile of hillside along Interstate 5, vast fields of ranunculas, gladiolus, and other flowers explode into vivid waves of red, yellow, orange, and pink, from mid March through early May, attracting thousands of spectators. Besides the blooming of the flower fields and accompanying springtime celebrations, Carlsbad puts on the largest street fair in the state, every May and November. Patrolling the huge crowds of people who browse more than eight hundred arts and crafts booths downtown are locals dressed as Keystone Kops, who help find lost parents and direct befuddled shoppers.

Surfers greet the dawn below the Oceanside pier, the longest wooden pier on the West Coast—1,949 feet long, built in 1888.

The sun and the waves break together on Oceanside Beach.

Vivid waves of rununculas and other blooming bulbs cascade across the countryside every spring in North San Diego County. Between mid March and May, nearly two hundred thousand people turn out to stroll through the flower fields.

WILDLIFE

Four-footed and finned animals are at home throughout San Diego County. Many thousands of rare and exotic specimens are on view at SeaWorld San Diego on Mission Bay, at the San Diego Wild Animal Park in north San Diego County (near Escondido), at the San Diego Zoo in Balboa Park, and at the Birch Aquarium at Scripps. At the top of La Jolla Bay, the aquarium resides in a eucalyptus forest setting. Kids and parents wander around outside, playing in the you-can-touch tide pools and picnicking beside the two-story-tall whale sculptures. Exhibits are filled with marine life in traditional, small glass exhibit tanks.

Best known as the home of Shamu, the killer whale, SeaWorld is a marine-themed aquarium and amusement park where visitors see and interact with common sea creatures and endangered species such as manatees and sea turtles. Some visitors have the chance to swim with dolphins and touch whales and other animals. Among the nearly four hundred species of fish here are Pacific seahorses, rarely seen in aquariums, and the roughjaw frogfish, called an anglerfish because it has a fishing "lure" that it waves in front of its mouth to attract other fish. It then rapidly opens its large mouth, sucking in the prey. In the Penguin Encounter, a moving sidewalk moves through a glassed-in replication of a patch of the Arctic, where hundreds of emperor penguins slip and slide in their icy habitat.

Animal rescue and rehabilitation are important parts of the park's operation. Beached and injured marine mammals, birds, and amphibians, including sea lions and elephant seals, are treated and released back into the Pacific. One of the famous temporary visitors was an orphaned, beached California gray whale named J. J., who was rescued, treated, and released by SeaWorld scientists.

SeaWorld's orca breeding program is the most successful in the world, with eleven healthy calves born here so far, including the grandchild of Shamu, the second generation of its species born in captivity. Other successful births have included rare Commerson's dolphins, Pacific walruses, and beluga whales.

At the San Diego Wild Animal Park, nearly four thousand animals live in surroundings similar to their native Asia and Africa. Visitors can ride a monorail, the better to get around the park's two-thousand-plus acres, and watch rhinos blithely lumber past herds of delicately striped impala, giraffes wander alongside cape buffalo, and lions sleep alongside elephants.

First established in the 1920s to house animals remaining from the Panama-California International Exposition, the San Diego Zoo is one of the most beautiful and largest zoos in the world. Characterized by a lack of cages, the animals live in moated, open, natural settings and in huge, walk-through aviaries.

The furry, white stars of the Polar Bear Plunge share the same two acres as Arctic foxes, snowy owls, and reindeer. Hippos swim in a 150,000-gallon pool with a glass window for viewing. Komodo dragons are required to keep to themselves, lest they devour their companions. The Giant Panda Research Station features Hua Mei, a cub born at the zoo in 1999 to Bai Yun, a female on loan from the Wolong Giant Panda Conservation Centre in China.

Visitors have the unique opportunity to ride open-air vehicles and moving staircases, to save energy for the miles of walkways and gain dramatic overviews of the sprawling zoo. It takes at least two days to see it all, from the butterfly hothouse to the rare Malaysian sun bears, the pygmy chimps, and the Gorilla Tropics exhibit.

Mike Shaw oversees the "Shark Experience" display at SeaWorld San Diego.

Mike Shaw, Curator of Fishes

Mike Shaw has worked at SeaWorld San Diego, the marine-themed aquarium and amusement park, longer than any other member of the staff. He signed on in 1964 as a fish cutter, preparing food for the animals. Later he became an aquarium supervisor, and in 1984 was promoted to "Curator of Fishes." Today Shaw oversees the care and feeding of nearly four hundred species of reptiles, amphibians, fish, and invertebrates, including those in the Shark Encounter, the tide pool and reef exhibits, and the freshwater and marine aquariums.

"I walk through the park and all the exhibits every morning, first thing, and consult with the aquarists, and I like to take another tour later in the day, when visitors are in the park," Shaw said. "Everyone is blown away by the Shark Encounter, where you are right there with the animals, swimming all around you in a clear tunnel. People really study the graphics, and they walk through, pointing out what they've learned."

"Children, especially, are very excited about touching the bat rays in the Forbidden Reef," he said. "The rays feel kind of rubbery and mucousy, but not slimy,

and they grow here up to about 140 pounds."

Although Shaw claims that fish are not known for their personalities, he is often followed along the glass aquarium windows by the puffers and triggerfishes, who seem to have an awareness. He said, "My favorites are the Napoleon wrasses. It is a tropical fish, a predator that gets quite large, perhaps two hundred pounds or better and a length of six feet, and is a popular for food in the Orient. Juveniles tend to be light or yellowish green, with large adults being purplish brown and blue, with a prominent hump on top of the head and large teeth."

Shaw and his colleagues believe that visitors to SeaWorld come away with more than just the memory of a fun day at a theme park.

"We work to instill in our guests a conservation ethic, and a realization that the resources of the sea, while vast, are not limitless," he explained. "I hope that our guests increase their empathy for . . . the marine animals that inhabit our planet. . . . I think that the opportunity to touch a bat ray or to see sharks in their own environment helps our guests to appreciate these animals."

ACKNOWLEDGMENTS

KAREN MISURACA

Without Michael's love and unending support, *The California Coast* would be an unrealized dream. In his usual selfless manner, he contributes greatly to all of my accomplishments.

Much gratitude to Gary Crabbe, a true artist whose images of California are nothing less than breath-taking, and whose good nature and capacity for hard work are to be admired.

Brian Huff of Ocean Futures is a good guy for his ready response and assistance. The California Coastal Commission is to be commended for their superb guide to every inch of the coast and their tireless efforts to provide and maintain access for all of us.

Thanks and much good luck to Todd Berger.

And many, many thanks to Amy Rost-Holtz, the soul of patience and an inspired, incomparable editor.

GARY CRABBE

I owe the greatest debt of thanks first to my wife, Connie, and to my mom, Gloria Crabbe, for they provided the greatest support and allowed me to take the time needed to photograph for this book. My thanks to Michelle Kingon and Phonh, whose helpful and trusted care of my son during the days while I was away made my travels that much easier.

I'd also like to thank all the people who kindly allowed me to take their pictures as I wandered this magnificent coast. To all of my "models," who were so gracious and understanding, you made shooting this book a wonderfully personal experience, even if our paths only crossed for a few brief minutes.

My thanks go to Lauren AshDonoho at the Hotel del Coronado; Lt. Christy Sheaff, U.S. Navy, PAO at the Commander Submarine Squadron Eleven; US Pacific Fleet, SUBASE San Diego; Frankie Laney at the Carlsbad Convention and Visitors Bureau; Kate Lister at Barnstorming Adventures Ltd. in Carlsbad; Amy Johnston at the Four Seasons Aviara; Gail Ossipoff at the Newport Beach Convention and Visitors Bureau; Shirley Davy at the Catalina Island Chamber of Commerce and Visitor Bureau; Cherryl Connally at Island Packers; Mary Ann Carson at the Cambria Chamber of Commerce; Ken Peterson at the Monterey Bay Aquarium, Val Ramsey at the Pebble Beach Company; the folks at Northern Air in Eureka for a great flight; and Joel Bahrenfuss for his open door hospitality, and for making the North Coast still feel like home. These people helped me capture much of the beauty and flavor of the California coast. The time, knowledge, directions, and accommodations they provided were invaluable.

Last but not least, I'd like to give special thanks to Galen and Barbara. If not for them, I would not be on the path I am now, nor would I be writing these words. I hope they know how much it all means to me.

BIBLIOGRAPHY

Alden, Peter, and Fred Heath. *National Audubon Society Field Guide to California*. New York: Alfred A. Knopf, Inc., 1998.

Arrigoni, Patricia. *Making the Most of Marin*. Fairfax, CA: Travel Publishers International, 2001.

Caughman, Erin, and Jo Ginsberg, eds. *California Coastal Access Guide*. Berkeley: University of California Press, 1997.

Dunhill, Priscilla, and Sue Freedman. *Glorious Gardens to Visit in Northern California*. New York: Clarkson Potter Publishers, 1993.

Dunn, Jerry Camarillo. *The Biltmore Santa Barbara, A History*. Santa Barbara, CA: Sequoia Communications, 1990.

Durrell, Lawrence. *Spirit of Place: Letters and Essays on Travel*. Stony Creek, CT: Leete's Island Books, 1969.

Earle, Sylvia A. *Sea Change: A Message of the Oceans*. New York: G. P. Putnam's Sons, 1995.

Eisen, Jonathan, Kim Eisen, & David Fine, eds. *Unknown California*. New York: Macmillan Publishing Company, 1985.

Gilbar, Steven, editor. *Natural State: A Literary Anthology of California Nature Writing*. Berkeley, CA: University of California Press, 1998.

Gilbar, Steven, and Dean Stewart. *Tales of Santa Barbara*. Santa Barbara, CA: John Daniel and Company, 1994.

Fong-Torres, Shirley. *San Francisco Chinatown: A Walking Tour*. San Francisco: China Books and Periodicals, Inc., 1991.

Lorentzen, Bob, and Richard Nichols. *Hiking the California Coastal Trail: Volume One*. Mendocino, CA: Bored Feet Publications, 1998.

McKinney, John. *Walking California's State Parks*. New York: HarperCollins West, 1994.

McMurtry, Larry. *Roads: Driving America's Great Highways*. New York: Simon and Schuster, 2000.

Meinkoth, Norman A. *The Audubon Society Field Guide to North American Seashore Creatures*. New York: Alfred A. Knopf, Inc., 1981.

Puterbaugh, Parke, and Alan Bisbort. *California Beaches*. Santa Rosa, CA: Foghorn Press, 1999.

Schama, Simon. *Landscape and Memory*. New York: Alfred A. Knopf, Inc., 1995.

Shanks, Bernard. *California Wildlife*. Helena and Billings, MT: Falcon Press Publishing Company, Inc., 1989.

Starr, Kenneth. *Material Dreams: Southern California through the 1920s*. London: Oxford University Press, 1990.

Udvardy, Miklos D. F. *The Audubon Society Field Guide to North American Birds, Western Region*. New York: Alfred A. Knopf, Inc., 1977.

Withey, Lynne. *Grand Tours and Cook's Tours: A History of Leisure Travel, 1750 to 1915*. New York: William Morrow and Company, Inc., 1997.

INDEX

About the Author and Photographer

Photo by Brad Perks

Karen Misuraca

Karen Misuraca is a travel and outdoor writer based in Sonoma, in the heart of California's Wine Country. She is the author of *The Insiders' Guide to Yosemite*, *CitySmart San Francisco*, *Quick Escapes from San Francisco*, and *Fun With the Family in Northern California*.

She contributes articles on golf and travel to a wide variety of publications, including *Alaska Airlines* magazine, TravelClassics.com, and others. She has written about golf in Spain, waterborne safaris in Africa, cruises in Costa Rica, and travel in Central America and Vietnam. She is often accompanied on her journeys by her daughter, Jessica, also a travel writer, and her partner, Michael Capp, an international broker of architectural products.

A lifelong resident of Northern California, Karen hikes, bikes, and kayaks the California coast with a lively contingent of grandchildren.

Gary Crabbe

Gary Crabbe has been capturing the majestic landscape of the western United States on film for the last ten years. His publication credits and clients include the National Geographic Society, the *New York Times*, the North Face, LL Bean, and the Nature Conservancy. His fine art photographic prints are included in both private and corporate collections.

His photographic career began with an elective course in black-and-white photography in college, but he soon found his real passion was the pursuit of color, light, and form in nature. He spent nine years as a photo editor and manager for a stock photo agency, during which time he also started his own photo company, Enlightened Images (www.enlightphoto.com).

Gary lives in San Francisco's East Bay, with his wife, Connie, and son, Brandon.